A Treasury of
Pennsylvania Tales

A Treasury of Pennsylvania Tales

Webb Garrison

RUTLEDGE HILL PRESS
Nashville, Tennessee

Published in Nashville, Tennessee, by Rutledge Hill Press, 211 Seventh Avenue North, Nashville, Tennessee 37219. Distributed in Canada by H. B. Fenn & Company, Ltd., 1090 Lorimar Drive, Mississauga, Ontario L5S 1R7.

Typography by E. T. Lowe Typesetting, Inc., Nashville, Tennessee.

Library of Congress Cataloging-in-Publication Data

Garrison, Webb B.
    A treasury of Pennsylvania Tales / Webb Garrison.
      p.   cm.
    Includes index.
    ISBN 1-55853-388-5 (pbk.)
    1. Pennsylvania—History—Anecdotes.   I. Title.
  F149.6.G37   1996
  974.8—dc20   95-50653
                                              CIP

Printed in the United States of America.

1 2 3 4 5 6 7 8 9—99 98 97 96

Contents

Introduction
Off the Beaten Path

One of the half-dozen most lethal explosions of the nineteenth century took place in what is now Pittsburgh. Few histories of the Keystone State mention the Allegheny Arsenal, despite the fact that fatalities in the 1995 Oklahoma City bombing were barely double those of the arsenal on a fateful day long ago.

Events and persons selected for treatment here are designed to lead you, the reader, off the beaten path. This means that in the case of well-known persons, relatively obscure or unfamiliar aspects of their careers are emphasized here.

Since hardly anything new can be written about Benjamin Franklin, it is his nearly forgotten son who occupies center stage in the Franklin story. Virginia was the birthplace of George Washington, yet Pennsylvania was the nucleus about which his military career revolved. An athlete-actor-author-musician whose name is familiar today got to the top by means of intelligence, ability, and hard work. He knows firsthand the meaning of racial prejudice, yet Bill Cosby is convinced that education will do more than legislation to lower racial and ethnic barriers.

Every Civil War devotee and most other people realize that without the determined involvement of Pennsylvania, it would have been difficult or impossible for Federal forces to win the Civil War. These days, hardly anyone remembers that a farmers' revolt in the state paved the way for the start of the Federal military effort.

Practically everyone realizes that Pennsylvania was geographically the keystone that held the northern and southern colonies together. Her central location in colonial America helps to account for her astonishing diversity and unequalled impact upon the fledgling United States of America. Even a careful look at today's maps often fails to reveal this all-important factor, however.

To the classroom student or the interested browser, twentieth-century maps give no hint that there were two early Pennsylvanias rather than one. Having only a few passes or gaps, the Allegheny Mountains literally bisect the state. Before the advent of gravel-surfaced roads, canals, and railroads, this formidable barrier separated the East from the West.

Dominating the eastern regions of the state, Philadelphia was a center of transportation, learning, government, and manufacturing. For a period, only London and New York exceeded it in size in the Western world. Yet at her western border, the state was literally—not figuratively—the U.S. frontier. No contemporary of John Bartram or William McGuffey knew that coal plus oil plus iron would eventually cause that frontier region to rival the East in wealth and influence.

Persons born in the Keystone State or who immigrated to it are as diverse as its geographical features. W. E. B. Du Bois, Chief Pontiac, and Molly Pitcher have only two things in common. All of them came to Pennsylvania from elsewhere— and each of them left behind a lasting set of footprints.

Nellie Bly, James Buchanan, and Mary Cassatt seem about as diverse as any three persons could be. Yet all three cherished their years in Pennsylvania, and each carved a bold signature into the bedrock of our nation.

Starting with a list of more than two hundred potential subjects, difficult and often painful deletions gradually reduced the number of Keystone State people and events to be treated here. Seeking for both diversity and freshness, I made these vignettes short and narrowly focused. Every chapter could easily be expanded into an entire book. If this collection holds your interest and to some degree enriches your understanding, it will have served its purpose.

"Awesome" is among the descriptive terms most applicable to Pennsylvania. May your exploration here yield both pleasure and fresh appreciation of a truly awesome set of men, women, and events.

Part One
Stranger Than a Soap Opera

Confederate Gen. Ambrose P. Hill approved a quest for shoes at first light on July 1, 1863. [NATIONAL ARCHIVES]

1
Gettysburg

No Soldier Is Stronger Than His Feet

Civilians around here don't like to talk. It took half an hour to find out that the shipment hasn't left."

"Did you find out anything about sizes?"

"No sir," replied a scout wearing a faded gray uniform. "But out of 150 or 200 pairs, some are bound to be usable. I think we ought to go for them."

Confederate Brig. Gen. J. Johnston Pettigrew nodded agreement but decided to ask the advice of his superior. A prewar attorney, the North Carolina native had originally refused to accept his commission because he lacked combat experience. On June 30, 1863, however, he was in command of a brigade in the division led by Maj. Gen. Henry Heth.

Heth already knew that a few scattered members of Federal cavalry units had been encountered earlier that day. When asked what to do about a supply of shoes now positively known to be in Gettysburg, he did not hesitate.

At his Cashtown headquarters he snorted, "No soldier is stronger than his feet," adding to Pettigrew, "Your barefooted men are in no condition to meet the enemy."

From his headquarters at a point about eight miles from Gettysburg, Heth took news of the shoes to his commander, red-shirted Maj. Gen. Ambrose P. Hill. "If there is no objection, I will lead my division into the town tomorrow and bring back a load of shoe leather," he said.

Nodding consent, Hill commanded, "Start at first light."

NEITHER OFFICER knew how fateful Hill's terse order would prove to be. Shortly before 5 A.M. on July 1 Heth's three divisions started toward Gettysburg, with Pettigrew's men last in the line of march. Three miles from Gettysburg by six o'clock, the Confederates caught occasional glimpses of church spires. About that time blue-clad vedettes were spotted, but they offered no opposition before withdrawing.

Approaching Willoughby Run, barely more than a mile from the town, Heth scanned a heavy growth of small trees. Since they provided good cover, he prudently ordered Maj. William J. Pegram to turn his artillery upon the knoll. Shells soon dropped among the trees without evoking response. Now confident, Heth ordered his men to occupy the town and seize the precious shoes stored there and awaiting shipment to a Federal depot.

The Confederates crossed the run, or stream, without incident and some of them started up the adjoining hill. Suddenly men in blue began firing from cover, then moved toward the enemy. Heth's men had encountered the famous Iron Brigade, a battle-hardened and superbly equipped unit made up of men from what was then known as the West.

Soon soldiers under Union Brig. Gen. John Buford trotted into action and the conflict became general. Members of the Ninth New York Cavalry joined the action, fighting on foot as was then customary among most horse-borne units. Just before or after eight o'clock, cavalryman Cyrus W. James took a direct hit and fell. His comrades did not realize that he was the first Union fatality of what was shaping up as a significant encounter.

As EARLY as June 12, Union scouts had reported that Robert E. Lee seemed to be moving toward the north-northwest with one hundred thousand men. Soon the Confederate general and Union counterparts knew that they would battle somewhere north of Maryland. No one, however, knew exactly where this conflict would take place.

Still ignorant of the location of the Army of the Potomac, on June 28 Lee's forces were dispersed over two thousand square miles of the Pennsylvania countryside. Abraham Lincoln had issued an emergency call for an additional fifty thousand volunteers who would strive to repel the invasion. Gov. Andrew

In an unusual move, Gov. Andrew Curtin issued an urgent call for volunteers who would serve no more than one hundred days. [LIBRARY OF CONGRESS]

Curtin called for "every available man in the Keystone State to serve for 100 days." By then it was known that men in gray had reached Carlisle and were within a few miles of Harrisburg.

Conflicting sets of orders issued to Lee's subordinates early on June 29 created considerable confusion. By the evening of the following day, however, the invaders were largely concentrated between Chambersburg and Heidlersburg. Since Lee considered this thirty-square-mile area too big, he gave instructions designed to pull the units closer together. Maj. Gen. J. E. B. Stuart had taken his cavalrymen on a wide-sweeping raid. Their absence contributed significantly to Lee's ignorance concerning the disposition of enemy forces.

EXCEPT FOR a relatively small band of Heth's men, few if any on either side saw Gettysburg as a target. Described as "quiet and sleepy," the town of two thousand lay about eight miles north of the Mason-Dixon Line that marked the boundary between Pennsylvania and Maryland. Although laid out in a fertile

valley and known for its artisans who turned out superior carriages and leather products, Gettysburg was chiefly noted for
the presence of a theological seminary. Ten miles west of town,
ranges of South Mountain were almost impenetrable except at
the Cashtown pass. It was from this point that the Confederates poured into the little hollow where the town nestled.

Several days earlier a few Confederate units had passed
through Gettysburg and noted that a dozen roads converged
there. Maj. Gen. Jubal Early, later infamous for demanding ran-
soms from towns and receiving some, paused on June 26. To
the inhabitants of Gettysburg he promised not to level their
homes and shops if they would immediately bring him ten
thousand dollars in gold and silver.

Dr. David Kendlehart, head of the borough council, reported
to the Confederate commander with a heavy heart. The money
demanded was entirely out of the town's reach, he truthfully
informed Early. It was equally impossible, he said, to provide
one thousand pounds of salt, one thousand pairs of shoes,
seven thousand pounds of pork, and other assorted supplies in
lieu of the gold and silver stipulated as ransom. Some flour
and pork, along with a small quantity of shoes made by local
cobblers, were all that Kendlehart could offer.

Early scoffed at accepting such a pittance and rode off
without waiting to take charge of the town's portable assets.
Moving rapidly into York, he demanded and received payment of an "indemnity" of twenty-eight thousand dollars
from the larger city. One of his subordinates probably told
colleagues under the command of Heth about the availability
of shoes in Gettysburg.

AFTER THE early-morning clash on July 1 between Heth's Confederates and Buford's Federals, scouts quickly reported to the
commanders of larger forces. By ten o'clock it was apparent
that tens of thousands of fighting men would soon converge
upon the site where the foes had blundered into one another.

Buford had climbed into the cupola of the Lutheran Seminary to watch the action. From that vantage point he was
delighted to see the arrival of Maj. Gen. John Reynolds and his
forces. "There's the devil to pay here!" Buford reputedly yelled
to Reynolds while gesturing to indicate the position south of
town that he wanted his comrade to hold.

An on-the-spot sketch by Alfred Waud depicts Union Gen. John F. Reynolds as he was shot from his saddle. [LIBRARY OF CONGRESS]

Less than half an hour later, riding just behind men of the Second Wisconsin Regiment, Reynolds was wounded behind his right ear. The first of numerous generals who took enemy fire at Gettysburg, Reynolds died almost instantly. As soon as the battle ceased to rage, his body was taken to Lancaster for burial.

By then the casualty count from three days of carnage at the Adams County seat had passed fifty thousand men and was still climbing. A seemingly insignificant quest for a few dozen shoes of unknown size triggered the biggest battle ever fought on the North America continent.

For more about Gettysburg see chapters 21 (George G. Meade) and 29 (Winfield S. Hancock); the Mason-Dixon story is told in chapter 15.

2
Mary Cassatt

More Impressionist Art Is in the United States Than in France

I'd like to sign up for next winter's antique class."

A quizzical look from a clerk in the Pennsylvania Academy of Fine Arts prompted an explanation.

"I'm Mary Cassatt, and I will be sixteen next month."

"You don't look your age, and we don't take children in that class. But at sixteen you will be a young woman—and first on our list for the winter class."

Elated, the girl who wanted to become an artist in spite of her father's objections spent the summer reading about and studying published art. Her mother was not surprised at her acceptance. When she was talking about her plans earlier, Mary squinted her fine gray eyes in a signal that every member of the family knew to mean she had made up her mind.

In Paris more than thirty years later, Louisa May Alcott's sister formed a lasting friendship with this woman who was born in Allegheny City. Alcott's vivid letters were used by her famous sibling as the basis of a novel. In it, fictional Miss Cassal was "a grand woman full of genius, who but for her sex would have made a name before now."

By the time those thinly disguised lines were penned, the artist was the central figure in a long-running feud with the famous Paris Salon. World-famous judges selected paintings for its exhibitions, and art lovers throughout the Western world flocked to admire them.

After four years of instruction, Cassatt decided that many of her teachers had closed minds. She abandoned the formal study of art, launched out on her own, and spent years commuting between Philadelphia and Paris. By the time she became the protagonist of an unfinished Alcott novel, Mary had developed her own highly individualized technique.

Her first acceptance by the Paris Salon led to a period of ecstasy. The impact of this euphoria was almost as great as the frustration brought about by her first rejection.

ROBERT CASSATT, an opinionated nineteenth-century father who was ready for retirement at age forty-five, didn't want his daughter to make a career in art. Grudgingly, he once said he would have found a place for her in his brokerage firm if he thought she would take it. Most of all he wanted her to find a husband and to give him grandchildren. Sometimes he regretted having taken his family from the finest mansion in Lancaster, overshadowing the nearby home of James Buchanan. Had Mary remained there after her early years across the river from Pittsburgh, he reasoned, she might have been content to accept the role society then expected of women.

Philadelphia society was considered by her father to be at the root of Mary's rebelliousness. He may never have learned that his financial success that made possible an early trip to Europe was the real culprit. As a small girl his daughter stubbornly insisted on climbing to the top level of a tall building on a spring night. From her perch the child was awestruck by the vista. Sparkling in the clear air, the shimmering city seemed to belong to another world.

When she was introduced to the works of then-obscure French artists who said they were putting their impressions on canvas, Cassatt vividly remembered that magical night above the city. Without adopting the style of any artist who entered her circle of friends, she exhibited many of her works in impressionist galleries. For a time these privately funded enterprises competed with the Paris Salon.

Louisa Alcott was closer to the truth than she realized; had Mary Cassatt been male, she would have been accepted and hailed by the time she reached maturity. Since she was a

Mary Cassatt, as depicted by Edgar Degas, a fellow member of the impressionist movement. [DICTIONARY OF AMERICAN PORTRAITS]

woman and since impressionism had not yet captured the imagination of America, she found it all but impossible to sell her works.

Frequently frustrated and often angry, she was influenced by her close friend, James McNeill Whistler. Her paintings of women in the traditional roles involved in nurturing a family were followed by numerous paintings of mothers caring for children. A work she called *Lady at a Tea Table* eventually became treasured by the Metropolitan Museum of Art in New York, although the woman depicted was offended because she considered herself more beautiful than her portrait. *Gardner Held by His Mother,* showing a small boy in his mother's arms, later came to be a prized acquisition of the New York Public Library.

At the time these works were being produced, however, many viewers failed to appreciate them. Some critics asserted that the woman from Philadelphia was the central figure of a tragedy. Having no children of her own, they said, she relieved her inner agony by depicting mothers and children.

Long before she gained recognition as the premier female artist of the Western world, Cassatt learned to ignore her critics. Since there was little commercial demand for her work or for that of her impressionist friends, she became an unpaid salesperson.

While visiting in Paris, Mrs. H. O. Havemeyer of Philadelphia was entreated by Cassatt to purchase a pastel by Edgar Degas. Reluctantly her friend relinquished all of her spending money— five hundred francs—for the work. Eventually the Havemeyers purchased enough impressionist art to fill a gallery.

Meanwhile, Cassatt persuaded one of her brothers to become the second American patron of impressionism. His first purchase, made at his sister's insistence before he became president of the Pennsylvania Railroad, was a work by Camille Pissarro. Once launched, Cassatt's crusade never ended. One by one, relatives and acquaintances yielded to her and bought paintings and prints of her selection.

Her own place in the world of art, largely won after her death, is now secure. Scorning the term "impressionism," she insisted that she and her friends were "independents." Whatever her label, Mary Cassatt rose to the top in her field. In addition, the woman from Philadelphia was the informal sales agent of much of her colleagues' work. Due to her influence, French impressionists came to be better represented in the United States than in France.

Louisa May Alcott's story comprises chapter 22. James Buchanan, Allegheny City, and the Pennsylvania Railroad frequently appear in these pages.

3
Albert Gallatin

Senators Believed They Had Silenced a Foreign Upstart

Assembled members of the U.S. Senate were divided on major political issues. Even over the minor issues, some strongly resented what they termed "pretensions of a foreign upstart."

Albert Gallatin, elected to the Senate by the Pennsylvania legislature in February 1793, didn't come quietly to the national capital in Philadelphia. Soon after his arrival, the freshman lawmaker introduced a bill demanding a detailed accounting from the secretary of the treasury.

Furious, Alexander Hamilton contacted friends who knew that the man born to a distinguished Swiss family had taken his oath of allegiance to his adopted country in October 1785. An article of the U.S. Constitution stipulates a senator must have been a citizen for at least nine years. By a February 18, 1794, vote of fourteen to twelve, Gallatin's name was purged from the rolls of the body to which his fellow Pennsylvanians had elected him.

Hamilton gloated that he would have no more demands for "unexpected and distressing calls for lengthy and complicated statements." When he made that pronouncement he could not have known that the man from Switzerland would hold the office of secretary of the treasury longer than any other man in the history of the country.

LEFT AN orphan at the age of nine, Gallatin found that he had rich and powerful relatives. As he neared maturity, they exerted their influence on his behalf. As a result, he was offered a commission as lieutenant colonel of a Hessian mercenary regiment that would soon go to America to help put down the colonial rebellion.

Gallatin haughtily rejected the commission but decided to go to America as a civilian. Through Benjamin Franklin, then at the French court in Versailles, he received a letter addressed to the son-in-law of the Sage of Philadelphia. Carrying a document written for Richard Bache and a letter from Lady Juliana Penn to John Penn, the nineteen-year-old crossed the Atlantic on the ship *Kattie.*

Legends to the contrary, he was never a freedom fighter. Years later he explained his decision to come to the new country in two sentences: "As I am lazy, I like a country where living is cheap; and as I am poor, I like a country where no person is very rich."

Although poor until he received his inheritance at age twenty-one, he must have been joking when he described himself as being lazy. No high-ranking U.S. official ever worked harder or longer after entering a president's cabinet.

Following a brief stay in Maine and Massachusetts, Gallatin found abundant cheap land available near the junction of the Monongahela River and George's Creek. Near this site, about four miles above the Virginia border, the adventurer built a log cabin and a general store.

Years earlier a tall Virginian came through the region. Engaged in selecting a route for a road across the "Alleghanies," as the name of the mountain range was then spelled, George Washington spent a few hours near the site at which Gallatin built his home in New Geneva. Gallatin called his home Friendship Hill. Later regionally famous, Friendship Hill was visited by the Marquis de Lafayette when he returned to America.

Citizens of Fayette County soon sent the newcomer with a French accent to the legislature. Members of that body then decided that he was just the right man to occupy a seat in the U.S. Senate. When he was ejected from the Senate, fellow Pennsylvanians responded in 1795 by sending him to the House of Representatives.

During some of the most chaotic years of the young nation's life, Gallatin became acquainted with a colleague from the South. This tall and lanky fellow who wore his hair in a queue tied with eelskin was scorned by many as a backwoodsman.

Gallatin's primitive log cabin was replaced by a splendid home on his "Friendship Hill."

Gallatin befriended the fellow and soon became close enough to him to call him Andy Jackson.

Acknowledged as a leader of what was then known as the Democratic Party—adamantly opposed to dominant Federalists—the man from New Geneva was reelected time after time. It was Gallatin who masterminded a plan, secretly shared with Thomas Jefferson, by which Aaron Burr was defeated in the 1800 presidential election. By that time members of the minority party in which he was a leader were calling themselves Republicans rather than Democrats.

Soon after taking over the reins of government, Jefferson persuaded the naturalized citizen to become his secretary of the treasury. Neither he nor the new president then anticipated that he would set a lasting record, heading the financial arm of the federal government for a dozen years.

During his tenure it became a standard practice to submit annual reports of the type Hamilton considered inappropriate. Because of Gallatin's influence, the House of Representatives established "a standing committee on finance." Soon it became

Albert Gallatin, scorned by Henry Clay as being "an alien at heart," was still an influential political leader at the age of eighty-six. [BRADY STUDIO, NATIONAL ARCHIVES]

the Ways and Means Committee, one of the most influential of congressional bodies even to this day.

It was Gallatin who made it possible to fulfill an agreement reached with the French by Jefferson. Without congressional authorization, the chief executive promised to pay nearly three cents an acre for an immense region stretching from the Mississippi River to the Rocky Mountains, from the Gulf of Mexico to what is now the Canadian border. Famous as the Louisiana Purchase, the deal doubled the size of the United States but was unfunded when the international agreement was made.

Interest on the new national debt ran to about seven hundred thousand dollars annually, an immense sum in 1803. Financier Gallatin devised legislation by which money to pay for Jefferson's purchase was funneled from annual duties on merchandise imported from abroad.

Gallatin was the only foreign-born cabinet member ever to guide the nation's financial affairs for three terms. After serving under Jefferson and Madison, he could have gone to Friendship Hill for relaxed years of retirement. Instead, he helped negotiate peace with Great Britain after the War of 1812.

In an era when a man of fifty-three was often considered to be old, the native of Switzerland said that his adopted country still needed him. Hence he served for more than a decade as an ambassador, first to France and then to Great Britain.

After he left public life, his friend John Jacob Astor persuaded him to go to New York. Astor induced him to head the new National Bank that later became the Gallatin Bank. In that post, he condemned the adoption of a high protective tariff.

When Pennsylvanians voiced their opposition to a 1794 tax on liquor, the so-called Whiskey Rebellion, Gallatin at first supported his fellow citizens but then later helped to suppress the movement. At the age of eighty-four, addressing an angry crowd, he voiced his strong opposition to the annexation of Texas. He helped to found the University of the City of New York and became the first president of the New York Historical Society.

Henry Clay scornfully described him in print as still being "an alien at heart," but Gallatin did not respond to the attack. Everyone on the national political scene knew that the Senate had deceived itself by thinking its actions in 1793 had silenced "a foreign upstart from Pennsylvania."

Both the tariff and the Texas issue figure largely in the George M. Dallas tale in chapter 18. Chapter 36 is devoted to the story of the Whiskey Rebellion and its unforeseen impact many years later.

4

Andrew Carnegie

The Day of Wooden Bridges Is Over

Abraham Lincoln paced nervously in the War Department telegraph office on Sunday afternoon, July 21, 1861. Beginning at 1:30, at fifteen-minute intervals he read messages dispatched from Fairfax Station, Virginia. At 3:30 the president received the terse final word from the first real battle of the Civil War: "Our army is retreating."

Trains packed with wounded men were already on the way to Alexandria from Manassas Junction. When the last of the men wounded at Bull Run were packed into boxcars, the weary civilian telegrapher climbed into the locomotive for the jolting journey. Earlier, he had ridden in the locomotive of another train that pulled the first contingent of volunteers into Washington City.

Andrew Carnegie was accustomed to hard work, but he had never been so tired before. Perhaps it was the stifling Virginia heat that made him wish he were not involved in what now seemed likely to be a long and bitter struggle, instead of the short conflict promised by the president.

An apparent sunstroke put Carnegie out of action for a few days. The assistant secretary of war, Thomas Scott, then came to his rescue. Handsome and refined, Scott had gone to work for the Pennsylvania Railroad in 1850 at the age of twenty-seven. Three years later, when he was placed in charge of the line from Altoona to Pittsburgh, he asked for and received a telegrapher.

Youthful Andrew Carnegie was locally noted as being the fastest operator of the O'Reilly telegraph system. After overhauling the lines in Scott's district, he became the private secretary to the superintendent. Hence the two had worked together for more than a decade before they found themselves in Washington. Lt. Gen. Winfield Scott was insistent in asking that they come to bring order out of the chaos of the military railroad system not yet fully functional.

In the aftermath of Bull Run, Scott put Carnegie in charge of establishing a military telegraph service. By the time it was beginning to operate well, Maj. Gen. George B. McClellan decided to reorganize his army and its support systems. That gave the telegrapher an excuse to return to Pittsburgh, where he took charge of the western division of the Pennsylvania Railroad.

Scott and other friends sent Carnegie numerous sketches and photographs of bridges that had been damaged or destroyed before, during, or after battles. As a result, in 1865 the expert telegrapher arrived at a reasoned conclusion: "The day of wooden bridges is over."

SON OF a hand-loom weaver married to a shoemaker, from his early childhood in Dunfermline, Scotland, Carnegie knew the meaning of hard work. At age thirteen he came with his parents to Allegheny, where Andrew soon found a job. Reporting about it to his father, he proudly said he'd start work the next morning as bobbin boy in a mill where he would make $1.20 a week.

Col. James Anderson took a liking to the small towhead who worked long hours in a cotton factory. Soon he made his personal library of four hundred volumes available to him. Although Carnegie didn't know it at the time, this act of kindness helped to change the direction of his life.

Reading made him ambitious, so at age fourteen Carnegie won a job as a messenger in a Pittsburgh telegraph office, doubling his salary to $2.50 per week. Within three years he became one of a handful of telegraphers who could distinguish letters by sound, so he was promoted to a key operator and his wages soared to $4.00 a week.

SOON AFTER the end of the Civil War, the man born in Scotland quit his railroading to form the Keystone Bridge Company. He dabbled in oil, sold securities on commission, and accumulated

One of Carnegie's early steel mills was named for Pennsylvania Railroad executive J. Edgar Thomson. [GEORGIA HISTORICAL SOCIETY]

what to him seemed to be a small fortune. With money in the bank and his heart full of hope, in 1873 he decided to concentrate upon the manufacture of steel.

This move affected not only the thirty-eight-year-old Carnegie and his future workers, but also the entire development of his adopted nation. Once the citizen of Pittsburgh made that crucial decision, the industrial supremacy of the United States was born.

Immense bodies of iron ore and vast regions rich with coal were familiar to everyone in western Pennsylvania. Until Carnegie envisioned bringing the two natural resources together, no one had seriously attempted to make the most of these resources.

The success of the new venture was immediate and spectacular. Soon the maker of steel was proud to name a new mill for J. Edgar Thomson, long-time superintendent of the Pennsylvania Railroad. By 1890 the Homestead mill built by Carnegie was famous throughout the Western world. Because of the impetus given to Pittsburgh by Carnegie, the river city became the iron and steel center of the nation.

Aided by Henry Clay Frick and Charles M. Schwab, the one-time bobbin boy built a mammoth privately owned company.

Andrew Carnegie's first public gift financed a free bath house for residents of Dunfermline, Scotland. [U.S. STEEL CORPORATION]

When J. Pierpont Morgan's financing enabled the U.S. Steel Company to absorb it, Carnegie became one of the richest men in the world.

Soon Carnegie articulated his personal philosophy: "A man should spend the first half of his life making money so he can spend the second half giving it away." His first public gift, free baths for Dunfermline, was made soon after the Thomas steel mills went into production in 1873. Once the spigot was opened, his stream of contributions gained speed and size with every passing year.

Mindful of what Anderson's generosity had meant to him, the steelmaker adopted a special motto. In great cities and in small towns, one Carnegie library after another challenged citizens with the message, "Let there be light." At a time when the purchasing power of one dollar was roughly equivalent to that of thirty or forty dollars today, Carnegie gave more than $350 million to libraries, colleges, a hero fund created by him, and numerous other causes.

Sparse records fail to indicate precisely how much money was made for its founder by the Keystone Bridge Company. One thing is clear, however. During 1861–65 civilians on both sides burned and blew up bridges almost indiscriminately. So did soldiers in both blue and gray. Their zeal showed that every wooden bridge was highly vulnerable.

Without the insight gained from seeing the destruction during the years of civil war, the Pennsylvanian by choice might never have left the business of telegraph lines and railroads. Had he not done so, the saga of the Keystone State and of the United States would not be what it is.

George B. McClellan's story is told in chapter 34; Abraham Lincoln and the Pennsylvania Railroad are central to several tales.

5

W. E. B. Du Bois

Eighteen Months in the Seventh Ward

Philadelphia was having a spasm of reform that called for a thorough study. To most white citizens the underlying cause was evident: the corrupt, semicriminal vote of the Negro Seventh Ward.

Everyone agreed that the cancer lay here, but an investigation under the imprimatur of the University of Pennsylvania was desirable. Hence Samuel McCune Lindsay of the Department of Sociology put his finger on me for the task.

Condensed and slightly adapted, that's the way a Harvard man described his earliest academic job after having received his doctorate. W. E. B. Du Bois, the university's first black Ph.D., was a master of biting sarcasm that has not lost its sting after nearly a century.

University of Pennsylvania records indicate that he came to Philadelphia as the recipient of a special fellowship that paid him nine hundred dollars a year. Afterward, Du Bois sometimes insisted that he was given the rank of assistant instructor at only fifty dollars per month. As he later recalled, these eighteen months that affected the course of his later life contained no contact with students and little with any member of the faculty. He had arrived knowing that he would have no role in the classroom.

As he understood it, his job was to analyze areas in which high-level discrimination existed. It was hoped that he would

30

accumulate a database that would help the city leaders open new doors for its black citizens. Hence the title used by the university provost to designate the pioneer research worker was accurate: Investigator of the Social Conditions of the Colored Race in This City.

Earlier, Du Bois had arrived at a conclusion he believed would stand the test of time. He was sure that the "Negro problem" would disappear in the light of systematic analysis. According to him, "wrong thinking about race" was based upon ignorance.

Philadelphia appeared to offer an opportunity to underscore truth instead of falsehood. He reached the city in 1896 with the announced intention of "finding out what was the matter with the Seventh Ward" so that cures could be devised for its ills.

Instead of seeking a place in university housing, he decided to move into the most turbulent area of the city. Most citizens knew that it was home to about 20 percent of Philadelphia's black residents. Marked by poverty and crime, it had a continuous two-hundred-year history. Du Bois and his wife found a single room over a cafeteria in what he considered to be the worst part of the Seventh Ward. Later he described the neighborhood at Seventh and Lombard Streets:

> In an atmosphere of dirt, drunkenness, poverty and crime the police were our government and murder perched on our doorstep. Kids played "cops and lady bums," a game of their own invention. When gunfire was heard in the night, you didn't try to get up lest you might find that you couldn't.

Du Bois devised a set of questionnaires, then went house-to-house for interviews. Many residents of the Seventh Ward received him with unconcealed suspicion, but only a dozen refused to talk with him. In an 1897 paper that grew out of his work in Philadelphia, he included an inner dialogue, part of which said: "What, after all, am I? Am I an American or am I a Negro? Can I be both? Or is it my duty to cease to be a Negro as soon as possible and be an American? . . . Does my black blood place upon me any more obligation to assert my nationality than German or Irish or Italian blood would?"

When not knocking on doors or musing about his identity,

he raged at prevailing attitudes among Ivy League colleges and universities. Harvard, he fumed, would never have thought about giving him even the low-level post provided by the University of Pennsylvania.

Working long hours, he accumulated what he considered to be a satisfactory body of evidence. In 1899 it was published as a ponderous volume entitled *The Philadelphia Negro: A Social Study.*

Once he completed his work and made his findings public, Du Bois expected many doors to open. When they did not, he went public with his frustration and anger. For the next quarter-century, he later charged, neither Washington nor "a single first-grade college in America gave any considerable scientific attention to the American Negro."

INCREASINGLY DOUBTFUL that any amount of study would yield solutions for the "Negro problem," Du Bois became a crusader.

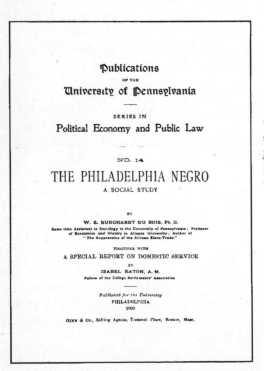

The title page of the book in which Du Bois reported the findings of his pioneer study. [UNIVERSITY OF PENNSYLVANIA]

Thinking that perhaps an international approach would be productive, he helped to plan and to lead Pan-African Conferences that were first held in England in 1900. This movement lasted nearly half a century but was never taken seriously by the world at large.

Having joined the faculty of Atlanta University, he taught economics and history while continuing to plan sociological studies and to cry for change. His most significant impact may have come from his role as a founder of the National Association for the Advancement of Colored People (NAACP).

He didn't like to admit it, but he couldn't escape recognizing that work such as he did in Philadelphia would never bring an end to the "Negro problem." Redirecting his life as a result of that conclusion, Du Bois spent twenty-five years as director of publicity and research for the NAACP. Soon after he took his new post, he founded and began editing a magazine whose title, *The Crisis*, suggests the nature of its contents.

As editor of The Crisis, *Du Bois discovered that a few paragraphs could stir up a hornet's nest.*

After World War I, Du Bois issued a strident call for democracy. His blistering lines in *The Crisis* denounced lynching and disenfranchisement of citizens. Calling the United States "a shameful land," he charged the federal government with responsibility for ignorance about blacks and for insults to them. Some of the many race riots of 1919 were said to have stemmed from that editorial.

During the presidential campaign of 1912, Du Bois corresponded with candidate Woodrow Wilson and worked for his election. When the twenty-sixth president failed to endorse plans to desegregate military units supposedly fighting to make the world safe for democracy, Du Bois exploded. He charged that the Virginia-born chief executive was not interested in the Negro race and did not desire to bring about any changes.

If by then the doctor of philosophy was beginning to revel in stirring up controversy, he never quite admitted it. Yet he paid an extensive visit to the Soviet Union in 1926, when "Red" was becoming a threatening word. Early in the life of the United Nations, through that body he appealed to the world to help abolish "Jim Crow in the United States."

Charged in 1950 with being "an unregistered foreign agent," Du Bois went on trial and won acquittal. Before the decade ended he made extensive trips to both the Soviet Union and to China. Back home, he soon joined the Communist Party. Then he left the United States and took up residence in Ghana, where he became a citizen at the age of ninety-five.

Dr. W. E. B. Du Bois was not buried in the city of his birth, Great Barrington, Massachusetts. His remains did not go to a cemetery populated with fellow graduates of Harvard, the University of Pennsylvania, or Atlanta University. Obedient to his wish to make a final symbolic gesture, in 1963 he was given a state funeral at Accra, Ghana, and was interred there.

6
George Catlin

Doors of Mystery Were Opened by a Portrait

Old Bear, or Mah-To-He-Ha, did not have to speak. His facial expressions and gestures showed that he was immensely pleased. As depicted by artist George Catlin, the medicine man of the Mandan Indians was wearing ceremonial clothing. To a trained eye it was easy to identify among his vestments several sacred plants and an otter skin.

Earth-lodge villages in North Dakota had never before been visited for any length of time by a white man. Absorbed with his goal of capturing Native American life on canvas, the artist ate and dressed like his hosts and had a working knowledge of their language.

Catlin rejoiced that his new portrait won approval because some of those whom he wished to depict had refused to be painted. Should they be captured on canvas, they said, they would become prisoners of the persons who held their likenesses.

Yet Old Bear readily consented to sit for Catlin and was inordinately proud of his portrait. To fellow tribesmen who saw the painting, he insisted that the white man's work constituted medicine, or magic.

That medicine was so potent, said the Mandan, that he wished to show his gratitude. He would permit the artist to watch an upcoming four-day *O-kee-pa* ceremony. Held annually, the mysterious rites were designed to ensure success to buffalo hunters and to make warriors of young males.

Catlin at work on the portrait that became a key by which doors of mystery were opened. [New York Historical Society]

The culture and appearance of the Mandans caused the occasional traders who had made brief contact with them before Catlin's 1832 stay to reach a strange conclusion. These tribesmen, concluded the few whites, were so fair of skin that they must be descendants of some lost Welshmen.

His painting having served as a key with which to open the doors of mystery, the man from the East was led into the big hut erected for the *O-kee-pa*. From the sidelines he watched as one intricate dance was followed by another. Finally, he saw and recorded his astonishment at the fortitude of fledgling warriors who had to endure lengthy torture to win acceptance by their elders.

His paintings and published accounts of men hanging in agony for hours were so vivid that many who saw them were skeptical. Just before the outbreak of the Civil War, Catlin's story and paintings came under fire. David D. Mitchell, once a fur trader, declared that the ceremonies described and depicted came from the imagination of the artist. Not until many years later was the Mitchell attack recognized as itself being fraudulent.

BORN AT Wilkes-Barre when the United States was only a decade old, Catlin was very early fascinated by stories his mother told. At age seven Polly Sutton had been captured by tribesmen of the Iroquois Confederacy and held prisoner for weeks. Although she was in an Indian village during the Wyoming River Massacre of 1778, Polly was later released unharmed.

Western Pennsylvania, then frontier country, saw at least fifteen Indian uprisings on a scale large enough to be known as massacres. Growing to maturity in the Susquehanna Valley of New York, where his family had moved, Polly's son was told the legends and tales of Indians, instead of children's stories brought from Europe.

Although he had little enthusiasm for it, Catlin followed his father's example and set himself up in Luzerne County as a lawyer. During trials, fellow attorneys noticed that Catlin amused himself by sketching persons in the courtroom. So many of his subjects wanted to buy his work that the young lawyer put aside his law books and moved to Philadelphia to paint miniature portraits.

These and his oil paintings brought him a comfortable living and contact with persons already notable or soon to be. Gov. DeWitt Clinton of New York sat for him; so did the future U.S. senator, Sam Houston, and future first lady Dolley Madison.

Yet February 24, 1824, was a day so notable for him that it was not eclipsed until Old Bear led him into the Mandan medicine lodge. On that date he was elected to the membership of the Pennsylvania Academy of Fine Arts. At the age of twenty-eight, Catlin could then demand and receive substantial fees for his work.

Instead of rejoicing at his growing reputation and income, the artist saved his money and made plans. Soon, he told himself, he could fulfill a dream he had cherished since childhood. He would go where the fast-vanishing Native Americans were to be found and would capture their faces and customs on canvas. His goal was to fully depict Indian leaders and Indian life so they would not be lost.

Osceola, the Seminole chieftain whose appearance would be unknown were it not for Catlin. [ENGRAVING AFTER CATLIN PORTRAIT]

George Catlin, probably as he appeared when exhibiting his Indian gallery in Europe.

Small, wiry, and largely self-taught, the man determined to preserve Native Americans with pigments worked with single-minded passion. He turned out more than three hundred oil portraits, one of which was the only known likeness of Osceola, last of the Seminole chieftains. Ceremonies, dances, games, and villages were the subject of more than two hundred more works. Buffalo hunts, central to the life of many tribes, were frequently and vividly depicted.

Unwilling to part with what he now saw as a unique collection, the artist put his work on exhibition in rented galleries. After touring cities of the Northeast, his Indian gallery traveled on to London and then Brussels and Paris. When interest lagged, Catlin began to offer live performances by Native Americans.

British and European interest in the Indian gallery far exceeded that generated in the land of its origin. So many people came to see his exhibitions that the artist was able to publish a two-volume book.

Packed with about three hundred engravings, his *Manners, Customs, and Condition of the North American Indians* drew little reaction from scholars. When twenty-five selected lithographs appeared in book form, they won praise from the general public but were largely ignored by his fellow artists and by art critics.

GEORGE CATLIN was sure that his life-shaping goal had been achieved; future generations would see lost cultures through his eyes. Yet when some of the Ojibwas who performed in his gallery died of smallpox, his expenses threatened to exceed his revenues.

Somehow he managed to make lengthy trips to South America and to the Pacific Northwest to paint Aucas, Connibos, Yumas, Apaches, and other tribesmen. His physical strength nearly exhausted and his artistic talent waning, he returned to the region of his childhood and early manhood. Months of knocking on doors proved futile; he could not sell his paintings.

WHEN HE died in 1829, James Smithson, a British scientist and natural son of the first duke of Northumberland, had left much of his fortune to the United States. Nearly twenty years went by before Congress decided to use the gift to establish the Smithsonian Institution in Washington.

Physicist Joseph Henry, first secretary of the Smithsonian, was fascinated by electricity and knew little about art or aboriginal cultures. Still, he realized that art works once included in the traveling Catlin gallery had no counterpart. As a result, he acquired the main body of the work of a nearly destitute artist who could have achieved and maintained financial success had he remained in Philadelphia.

Today the Smithsonian's Catlin Gallery is a focus of interest for scholars and for visitors from throughout the world.

7

Percival Drayton

At Port Royal It Was Brother Against Brother

Cmdr. Percival Drayton went from one desk to another in the headquarters building of the Philadelphia naval base on February 25, 1861. Eventually he found the official responsible for maintaining the register of personnel.

Introducing himself, Drayton explained that he was on ordnance duty at the big navy yard. "You have me listed as a citizen of South Carolina," he continued. "It is true that I was born there, but I want my record changed to show that I am now a citizen of Pennsylvania."

It would take a lengthy movement along the paper chain to do as the forty-eight-year-old requested. Yet willingness to initiate that process was almost instantly acknowledged. Like everyone else, the registrar knew that South Carolina now called itself an independent republic. That action was enough to make many officers try to sever links with the seceded state.

Cadets at The Citadel, the military academy in Charleston, had recently added injury to insult by firing on the supply ship *Star of the West*, which was trying to render assistance to the U.S. garrison at Fort Sumter. The ship withdrew, its mission a failure. After a lengthy bombardment a few months later, the garrison surrendered the fort to South Carolina's military. Small wonder then that the naval commander wished to renounce his birthplace officially.

A brother four years Percival's senior had attended West Point in 1824 and possibly influenced the younger Drayton to

41

*Gen. Thomas F. Drayton was
charged with the defense of
Port Royal.* [U.S. ARMY
MILITARY HISTORY INSTITUTE]

enter a different branch of military service. Appointed a mid-
shipman in 1827 at the age of fifteen, Percival began the slow
ascent up the chain of command.

WILLIAM DRAYTON, father of the two boys, was taken from
Florida to Charleston as an infant. Educated in England, he
returned to the South Carolina port and became a prominent
attorney.

During Percival's second year in the U.S. Navy, his father
delivered a stirring July 4 speech in Charleston. His outspoken
condemnation of the state's desire to nullify federal laws cost
him so many clients that he moved to Philadelphia. There he
soon became president of the Bank of the United States.

Percival maintained close ties with his father. His brother
Thomas, however, did not. After eight years in the U.S. Army,
he resigned his commission and took up residence in Drayton
Hall, now the central structure of a vast South Carolina plantation famous for its spring flowers.

In the threatening atmosphere just before the outbreak of
civil war, Percival could honestly say that Philadelphia had
been his home for nearly three decades. He knew that his deci-

Percival Drayton commanded one of the warships that attacked and defeated the Confederates at Port Royal. [NAVAL ARCHIVES]

sion to label himself a northerner could lead to his severing ties with relatives in the South. Yet he took the fateful step with no sign of mental reservation.

EIGHT MONTHS after turning his back upon his South Carolina roots, Percival learned that officials of his city took the growing North-South conflict very seriously. When trains from New York arrived at Philadelphia on August 22, 1861, marshals seized every copy of the *New York Daily News* because it had been labeled as subversive.

Two months later, the city council purchased a ceremonial sword that was presented to Maj. Robert Anderson, hailed in the North as the hero of Fort Sumter. A refreshment center set up close to Philadelphia's railroad depots was by that time serving more than a thousand Union soldiers every day.

Having been placed in command of the USS *Pocahontas* on October 9, Percival was ordered to patrol the Potomac River. This vessel, a screw-driven steamer, was rated as a second-class sloop. Since the preceding June, the ship's gunners had exchanged fire with Confederate shore batteries frequently. Since this mission was deemed vital to the safety of Washington, Drayton was surprised to be ordered south for blockade duty soon after taking command.

GIDEON WELLES, U.S. secretary of the navy, was fifty-nine years old and had no experience on the water. Yet when Lincoln announced that all Southern ports would be blockaded, Welles easily perceived a major problem. To implement the president's directive, he must have a supply and refueling base for naval vessels on duty below Cape Hatteras, North Carolina.

Steamers used huge quantities of coal, preferably of the smokeless or anthracite variety from the mines of Pennsylvania. Although readily available, it had to be stockpiled somewhere along the Confederate coast.

Welles and his subordinates studied reports of enemy strength in major ports and were discouraged. Wilmington, Charleston, Savannah, and Mobile were heavily defended; direct movement against one of them was out of the question for the present.

Inch-by-inch analysis of coastline maps eventually yielded a target. At Beaufort, South Carolina, the Broad and Beaufort Rivers converge to flow into an immense natural harbor. Bordered on one side by Hilton Head Island, Port Royal Sound was large enough for two dozen warships or more to anchor simultaneously. This location had an additional advantage: Port Royal was about midway between Charleston and Savannah, two likely targets for immediate Union action.

To take the base, the Federals would have to overcome two Confederate strongpoints: Fort Walker and Fort Beauregard. Together these Confederate bastions mounted forty-three heavy guns. A single naval vessel, the USS *Wabash*, carried fifty-two.

Maintaining strict secrecy, Welles succeeded in assembling eighteen warships and thirty-eight transports capable of carrying twelve thousand soldiers. By October 29 they were ready to set out from Hampton Roads, Virginia.

A fleet of twenty-five coal ships, ordered to assemble off the Georgia coast, was already under way. Additional steamers and frigates, earlier sent to Southern waters, were directed to join the expedition led by Com. Samuel F. DuPont. Except for

The bombardment of Forts Walker and Beauregard in Port Royal, South Carolina.
[GEORGE E. PERINE ENGRAVING]

him, no commander of a vessel knew that Port Royal was its destination until sealed orders were opened at sea.

ABOARD THE *Pocahontas*, Drayton and his men reached Port Royal on November 7. Hours before their arrival, DuPont's ships had begun circling the harbor and firing on the Confederate positions. In obedience to orders, Drayton dropped anchor. He then signaled for his gunners to make Fort Walker their only target and to fire as rapidly as possible.

Within two hours Fort Walker was abandoned and its commander had fled on horseback. Only after an overwhelming Federal victory was certain did Percival Drayton learn that Fort Walker had been commanded by Confederate Brig. Gen. Thomas Drayton. By that time, Union soldiers and sailors were busy destroying captured guns.

HUNDREDS OF families were divided in loyalty during the Civil War. As a result, brother against brother has come to be a taken-for-granted label for the conflict. Many sets of siblings fought on both sides, but few of them participated in the same battles. Drayton of Philadelphia was among the handful of Federal officers who actually fired upon a brother's post.

All evidence indicates that had Percival known that Thomas was in command at Fort Walker, he would not have altered his role in the battle of Port Royal.

James Buchanan's interrelationships with other Pennsylvanians were numerous and complex. He is mentioned frequently and is central to the story of Harriet Lane in chapter 19.

8
William H. McGuffey
An Aspiring Teacher Made the Nation His Classroom

Most fathers and mothers who heard that a school was opening near Pennsylvania's border knew nothing about the teacher. Nevertheless, they were delighted that the boys and girls living on the frontier would have a chance to get an education.

When forty pupils arrived on September 1, 1814, the schoolmaster had to find larger quarters. At age fourteen, William H. McGuffey had expected to attract only a handful of boys and girls, if any.

His mother, Anna, couldn't resist beaming as she said, "I told you so!"

Her pride and delight stemmed partly from the fact that she had given the boy most of his early schooling. Had she not taught him, he would have had little opportunity to learn at Claysville. Southwest of Pittsburgh and within walking distance of present-day West Virginia, the settlement was too small to attract a schoolmaster.

William began his own teaching in the larger village of Union, where more than two dozen families had school-age children. There's no record of how he proceeded to teach the three Rs. However, he must have been adept at readin', 'ritin', and 'rithmetic because word about him traveled nearly thirty miles to Darlington, where a minister operated Old Stone Academy.

The Reverend Thomas Hughes had classroom space to spare. In addition, he needed someone to sweep the church of

47

This may be the only portrait of William H. McGuffey. While teaching at the college, he spent most of his free time with children. [DICTIONARY OF AMERICAN PORTRAITS]

which he was pastor and to pull weeds from the yard. By offering William what might today be called a tiny scholarship, Hughes accomplished two things at once. He arranged to have the work done and he added another student to his little school.

In 1800 many sections around state borders were fuzzy and the clerks of court seldom kept birth records. Hence both Pennsylvania and Ohio have claimed the adolescent teacher. Regardless of where McGuffey was born, he studied Latin at Darlington, Pennsylvania. It was there that he decided to spend the rest of his life in the classroom. As a result, he attended a nearby college and stayed as long as he could. Named for the county in which it stood, Washington College was an Ivy League institution by comparison with many schools in Appalachia.

Determined to teach, McGuffey then opened a school in Paris, Kentucky. His lack of a diploma from Washington Col-

Lesson 45 of the First Reader *tells of Lucy's kindness to her parrot, Polly.*

lege didn't hamper his work aimed at inspiring boys and girls to study phonics and to become skilled in cursive writing.

Talk about the results achieved by the young teacher drifted all the way to Miami University in Oxford, Ohio. Soon the frontier idealist who spent many of his early years in the Keystone State became a professor.

At Miami University, McGuffey joined the faculty to teach "ancient languages," by which its president probably meant a smattering of Latin. Satisfied with his salary and prestige but restless for the classrooms he had left, the young professor invited the boys and girls of Oxford to his home. After a few of them had spent three or four afternoons with him in his back yard, they began coming in droves.

With students clamoring for his help, McGuffey was reluctant to tell them that no acceptable textbooks were to be had. Except for the old *New England Primer,* hardly anything designed for use by beginners was in print.

At some point his young students inspired him to prepare two small books, and a Cincinnati publishing house decided to issue McGuffey's *First Reader* and his *Second Reader*. The titles did not imply that they were intended for use in what we now call first and second grades. Instead, one was for beginners and the second took up where the first one left off. Eventually a set of six McGuffey readers and a spelling book were on the market.

SCORES OF elementary school textbooks are available today. Some have only a single printing while others are reprinted several times before going out of print. Despite what seems to be a superabundance of readers, thousands of boys and girls still turn to McGuffey's primers for instruction. Part of their staying power stems from the fact that even very brief lessons usually include a story that highlights a moral value.

Parents who support many private schools strongly believe that honesty, courage, and other qualities should be stressed along with reading and writing. Illustrations that are plain and simple by comparison with television images help to stress the values in which the man from Washington County believed so strongly.

Publisher's records indicate that at least two hundred thousand copies of McGuffey's little books have been distributed during the last 150 years. Many of them are used over and over, handed down to younger sisters or brothers.

Literally, not figuratively, the Pennsylvania boy who learned at his mother's knee succeeded in making the United States of America his classroom.

Part Two
Trailblazers

William Bartram, dressed for a lecture rather than for another foray into a distant forest. [DICTIONARY OF AMERICAN PORTRAITS]

9
John and William Bartram
Petals of a Daisy Launched a Century-long Quest

Red-Stick Creeks of Alabama signaled to the white man they had come to trust. Known to them as "Puc-puggy" and to white men of the southwestern frontier as "Billy the Flower Hunter," he nodded and followed their rapid steps.

Already he had been led by them to an immense stand of big trees not far north of present-day Mobile. To William Bartram of Philadelphia it seemed that the only proper name for the place was "the great high forests."

Clusters of oaks and hickories were punctuated by other giants. In a single day he had identified ash, sour gum, sweet gum, beech, mulberry, scarlet maple, black walnut, chestnut, and dogwood. Now it was obvious that the natives with whom he communicated largely by gesture had other wonders to show him.

Following a narrow trail, the party suddenly emerged into a large clearing. Around its circumference were sturdy vines hanging low from the weight of dark-purple grapes such as few white men had ever seen.

Because he found their taste musky-flavored, Bartram called these grapes muscadines. The choice of this name may have been influenced by one form of the name white men gave to his Creek friends. Describing muscadines found in Muscogulge country in his journal, he noted:

> They do not climb into high trees, but creep along from one low shrub to another. They extend their branches to a great distance

horizontally round about; and it is very pleasing to behold the
clusters pendant from the vine, almost touching the earth.

These huge and luscious grapes, apparently native to the
region and quite unlike any variety cultivated in the Old
World, had thick and tough skins. That made them prized by
Native Americans, who dried them "by first sweating them on
hurdles over a gentle fire, and afterward exposing their
branches to the air and the sun."

When word of the botanical discovery reached England, the
muscadine excited great wonder. "With 6,000 varieties of
grapes known and cataloged," one scientist wrote, "it is almost
beyond belief that an untrained American should have discovered a new one that is remarkably distinctive."

Following his father's example of traveling slowly on foot,
William explored what is now the southeastern United States
for four years beginning in 1773. Dr. John Fothergill, a prosperous Quaker, advanced funds to cover the expenses of the expedition. In return, numerous seeds, dried specimens, and
beautifully colored drawings eventually found their way to
Bartram's patron in England.

Not long after having returned to the city of his birth, the
botanist was elected to the American Philosophical Society.
Benjamin Franklin had organized it in 1743, with William's
father as a charter member.

Soon William began putting the finishing touches upon a
pioneer book about travel. He became famous after the 1791
publication of his *Travels through North and South Carolina, Georgia, East and West Florida, the Cherokee Country, the Extensive Territories of the Muscogulges, or Creek Confederacy, and the Country
of the Chactaws.* Few early books by an American excited similar interest abroad. After having been reprinted in London and
in Dublin, *Travels* was translated into German, then into Dutch
and French.

Although not much more than five feet in height, the man
from Pennsylvania loomed tall in the world of botany.
"Dressed from neck to foot entirely in leather," he had walked
a few miles nearly every day for forty months. In addition to
discovering the muscadine and a host of other new plants, he
penned careful descriptions of 215 kinds of birds and fishes.

Found near the Altamaha River in Georgia, Bartram honored a fellow Philadelphian by calling this flower Franklinia altamaha.

WILLIAM'S WORK, continued until his death at age eighty-two, was based upon that of his father, John. Tradition has it that as a boy of ten, John Bartram was plowing his father's field at Marple, near Darby, in nearly level country south of Philadelphia. His plow accidentally turned up a daisy, so the youngster stopped his horse to examine it. Amazed at the symmetry of its petals, he began to pluck and examine the blossoms and the leaves. As soon as he had money in his pocket, he walked to the city and bought a *Herbal,* a pioneer book about botany.

Before age thirty John Bartram had acquired land on the banks of the Schuylkill River just three miles from Philadelphia. There he laid out a carefully planned garden and attempted to cross-breed plants to produce hybrids.

Four stone houses, among America's earliest, were built in and around the garden. John's son, William, was born in one of them. In boyhood he became well acquainted with Benjamin Franklin and George Washington. Both often came to see what new wonders were to be found in America's first botanical garden.

Bartram's field drawing of the fish he knew as the white perch, or bream.

Correspondence with British scientists brought the elder Bartram to the attention of King George III. He was named botanist to the king, a post that carried with it a stipend of fifty pounds per year.

Using funds from this source, John Bartram made his way to a frontier fort near the modern-day site of Pittsburgh. Later, after having sailed to Charleston, he trudged through Georgia and much of Florida on foot.

As the fame of Bartram's garden spread, naturalists came from great distances to see it. Some of the trees he planted there were still thriving more than a century later.

Small wonder that from the time he was a toddler following in his father's footsteps, William had one clear goal in life. He would supplement and amplify the work of John Bartram and in the process would enhance the fame of the city where he was born.

During a quest that included two generations and stretched across 110 years, John and William Bartram never wavered from a goal said to have been inspired by a single daisy. Together they made Philadelphia a botanist's haven—long the best spot in the United States to study native flowers, shrubs, and trees.

10
Nellie Bly

Investigative Reporting Was Born in a Madhouse

Readers of the *New York World* blinked with astonishment on October 16, 1887. A single story filled page one of a new Sunday section, then jumped inside the paper and occupied most of the second page.

New Yorkers knew that Joseph Pulitzer was hungry for fame and fortune, in that sequence. They were accustomed to seeing in the *World* stories whose subject matter or treatment would have barred them for any "respectable" competitor. This time, though, Pulitzer had outdone himself. The headlines promised sensational revelations:

INSIDE THE MADHOUSE

Nellie Bly's Experience in the Blackwell's Island Asylum

How the City's Unfortunate Wards
Are Fed and Treated

The Terrors of Cold Baths and Cruel,
Unsympathetic Nurses

Attendants Who Harass and Abuse Patients
and Laugh at Their Miseries

*The title page of the 1887
booklet that made Nellie Bly
famous.* [LIBRARY OF
CONGRESS]

Two months later a slightly modified form of the reporter's
two-part account was published in book form. With its release,
investigative reporting was born. Although crude by the standards of Bob Woodward and Carl Bernstein's exposé of the
Nixon administration's Watergate scandal, it marked a water-
shed in journalism. A woman from rural Pennsylvania had
come a long way in a short time.

ELIZABETH COCHRANE was born in Armstrong County two years
after the Civil War. Like William McGuffey, her early education
was gained at home. At age thirteen she was sent to a normal
school not far away in Indiana, Pennsylvania. Before the term
was over, her instructors told her parents that time and money
were wasted upon Pink, as she now called herself. In their
opinion she would never become a teacher such as the school
aimed to produce.

A period caricature of George Madden, managing editor of the Pittsburgh Dispatch. [CARNEGIE LIBRARY OF PITTSBURGH]

After moving with her family to Pittsburgh a bit later, Pink turned red in the face when she scanned a newspaper article entitled "What Girls Are Good For." On the spur of the moment she dashed off an angry memorandum to the editor and signed it "E. Cochrane."

George A. Madden, managing editor of the *Pittsburgh Dispatch*, didn't expect the writer to appear at his door as the letter threatened. When eighteen-year-old Pink confronted him with green eyes blazing, she said she'd give anything in the world to get a chance to write for the newspaper. Madden not only decided to give her a try, he even told her to pick her own subject.

In her first piece, she wrote about a topic respectable folk seldom mentioned in public—divorce. Any husband or wife, Pink argued, ought to have the legal right to sever ties that had become oppressive.

Madden nodded approval as he scanned the manuscript. "I'm going to call it 'Mad Marriages' and run it," he told an aide. Informing Pink that she had a job at five dollars a week, he simultaneously informed her that her nickname was no good for a journalist.

Tradition says that someone in the newsroom was lustily humming a song by a Pittsburgh native. Madden caught the

Nellie Bly at the peak of her career.

melody, perhaps half-consciously, and on the spot adapted Stephen Foster's "Nelly Bly" into Nellie Bly.

After turning out one attention-catching story after another, Nellie spent five months in Mexico. Her articles for the *Dispatch* that exposed poverty and degradation in that nation became the 1888 book *Six Months in Mexico*. When it attracted far more purchasers than she had expected, Nellie decided that she was ready to hit a major newspaper.

When she arrived in New York, instead of being hailed as a minor celebrity, she found herself an unknown among strangers. No one at any of the city's six major newspapers showed any interest when she applied for work.

Determination and tear sheets of her stories from Pittsburgh, however, eventually led the *New York World*'s managing editor, John Cockerill, to give the young woman a chance. Since she was determined to write for New Yorkers, Cockerill told her, she could start with an assignment no one else wanted. If she could get herself committed to a ward on Blackwell's Island, she might find something that would interest the *World*'s readers.

When the newspaper had been purchased by Pulitzer in 1883, the circulation of the *World* had plummeted below twelve thousand. By the time Nellie joined the staff, it had climbed past two hundred thousand.

Successfully convincing a board of physicians that her sanity was suspect, the reporter spent ten days among women who had been diagnosed as deranged. Her exposure of the conditions within the asylum created such an outcry that a grand jury was convened to conduct an investigation.

Very pleased with herself, the woman from Pennsylvania readily signed a book contract with the John W. Lovell Publishing Company, which quickly issued a new edition of her book about

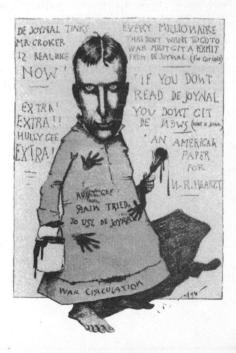

Pulitzer's rivals satirized him for his willingness to publish anything that would sell papers. [LIBRARY OF CONGRESS]

life in Mexico. The cover of the twenty-cent volume identified Nellie Bly as the author of the series "Ten Days in a Madhouse."

When Pulitzer moved his newspaper into new headquarters within a twenty-six-story skyscraper, he was more eager than ever to boost circulation. Revenue from the sale of papers at two cents per copy was inconsequential, but more readers meant more advertisers at higher rates. Muckraking was a sure way to attract readers as were sensational stories based on the personal experiences of writers. Thus he decided to capitalize on the popular novel by French author Jules Verne, who sent fictional Phineas Fogg around the world in an incredible eighty days. If the record established by a novelist could be beaten, tens of thousands of new readers would buy the *World*.

Nellie Bly was highly gratified but not especially surprised when she learned that she had been picked to better the time of Phineas Fogg. Before she could set off on her journey, however, a reporter from a competing newspaper joined in the contest, making it a true race. Now Nellie had to better the time of a flesh-and-blood opponent as well as Verne's fictional hero.

Soon after the race began in November 1889, the woman without training in journalism gained a small but significant lead. Gradually increasing it, she was given a heroine's welcome when she returned to New York in just seventy-two days.

Stories hastily written during Nellie Bly's race around the globe and dispatched from dozens of locations caused readers to scramble for copies of the *World*. With her birth name of Elizabeth Cochrane practically unknown, Nellie Bly became a national figure.

The story of Stephen Foster is given in chapter 27.

11
Bill Cosby

Education Beats Legislation Four Ways from Sunday

Johnneta B. Cole, newly inaugurated as president of Spelman College, flashed a smile to the audience of twelve hundred. Stepping to the podium, she held a memorandum in her hand but did not refer to it as she said:

Friends and supporters of America's oldest institution for higher education of black women, it gives me great pleasure to say that a special gift is being made to us. William and Camille Cosby are making available $20 million in a lump sum. Sixty percent of this unprecedented gift will be allocated to the Camille Olivia Hanks Cosby Academic Center. Forty percent will be set aside as an endowment for the benefit of the college.

When wildly enthusiastic applause began to subside, one of the nation's best-known entertainers took the microphone. Earlier he had delighted faculty members, alumni, and friends of the college with his wit and candor on a variety of subjects.

In almost casual fashion he explained why the gift, unprecedented in size among institutions founded for the education of African Americans, was being made:

Mrs. Cosby and I did not throw that gauntlet down to show off . . . twenty million can buy a whole lot of Rolls Royces. We decided to stop black Americans and international black folk

*William Henry
Cosby Jr., Doctor
of Education.*
[SPELMAN
COLLEGE]

from across the ponds from thinking small. I think we all understand that these schools need money, but I think we've accepted
that some white people are either going to keep them alive or
let them go. I want Johnneta Cole to understand the love that
Camille and I have for this college, the love that we have for the
women who, in spite of the odds against them, came to this
school to challenge themselves, to challenge the school, then to
challenge what we call "the outside world." This building is for
all those beautiful women.

Dr. Cole responded briefly but emphatically. "When the first
black family of America decides that there is no stronger statement than the need to well educate young black women," she
said, "you ought to let the *whole* church say Amen!"
    A long-time benefactor of Spelman who had seen other
administrators inaugurated noted that ties between the new
president and the award-winning entertainer were strong.

"Dr. Cole inspired him by her teaching when he was a student at the University of Massachusetts," he said. "His daughter's great experience as an undergraduate at Spelman hasn't hurt a bit."

Reflecting upon what was said and done early in November 1988, three days of speeches and celebrations were condensed into a single sentence by a wealthy benefactor: "Education beats legislation four ways from Sunday!"

That verdict does not mean that the big giver to higher education belittled the impact of legislation. Having experienced the full meaning of racial segregation, William Henry Cosby Jr. knows that some things have changed as a result of belated action in Congress and in state legislatures. Yet many longstanding barriers, tacitly accepted by white Americans, are for practical purposes still in place.

That night at Spelman it was clearly evident that Cosby is wholeheartedly committed to education as the highway to lasting progress. He was reared in a Philadelphia suburb where conditions were not much better than those of the area studied by W. E. B. Du Bois much earlier. His mother worked as a cleaning woman in the homes of prosperous whites so that her sons would have adequate food and clothing. Still the family had to accept relief, as welfare was called during the 1940s.

Nearly six feet tall at age fifteen and known to his friends as Shorty, Bill sold fruit on the streets, shined shoes, and worked in a grocery. Tests indicated that he was highly intelligent, so he was placed in special classes at Germantown High School.

Working up to forty-eight hours a week and playing ball in what little time was left over was too much for even a gifted student. Informed that he would be required to repeat the tenth grade, Shorty became a high-school dropout.

After he served a stint in the U.S. Navy, Cosby's unusually high degree of manual dexterity took him to college. Yet he could not have attended Temple University without the track-and-field scholarship awarded to him. Ernie Casale, athletic director of the university, was not surprised to hear that scout Emlen Tunnell of the NFL Green Bay Packers had looked Cosby over. Greatly impressed, Tunnel encouraged Cosby to consider a professional football career after graduation.

That sounded great to the young man from the projects in Philadelphia, but another opportunity soon took priority. At

Halfback and fullback Shorty Cosby, Germantown High School, Class of 1964.
[TEMPLE UNIVERSITY]

The Cellar, a Philadelphia coffeehouse, Shorty was offered five dollars a night to tend bar and crack jokes. He performed so well that he soon gravitated to Greenwich Village in New York. Faced with the choice of continuing his education or trying to make a good living as an entertainer, he dropped out of college.

FOR THE majority of people who put their education aside, there is no turning back. Bill Cosby, however, is cut of quite different cloth from most persons. Crediting him with life experience in lieu of a bachelor's degree, the University of Massachusetts at Amherst accepted him as a graduate student. It took four years for him to earn a master's degree. Not satisfied after receiving it, the two-time dropout with a national following stayed at Amherst to become a doctor of education. His wife also holds an earned doctorate that is rarely acknowledged except during academic ceremonies. By the time he became the star of The Cosby Show, he was an entertainment celebrity. Comparatively few who have seen The Cosby Show have read its credits carefully. There the entertainer is identified as William H. Cosby Jr., Ed.D.

Dr. Camille Cosby at groundbreaking ceremonies for the building that bears her name. [SPELMAN COLLEGE]

Along with a passionate belief in the importance of education, Cosby has continually stressed another factor he considers central to life. Each of his five children can testify to that concern on the part of the man who gave African American higher education its largest-ever single financial boost.

Erika Ranee, oldest of the Cosby children, is followed by Spelman alumnus Erinn Charlene, Ennis William, Ensa Camille, and Evin Harrah. Many persons are not aware that both Drs. Cosby are absorbed with the importance of "Excellence with a capital *E*." It's easy to overlook the role *E* for Excellence played every time Cos and Camille had to choose a baby's name.

SO MANY notables have been dubbed Renaissance men that the title has lost much of its meaning. Even if it were not threadbare, it would not be adequate to label the doctor of education from Germantown. Actor-athlete-author-benefactor-comedian-director-father-husband-musician-student Cosby has displayed excellence in almost a dozen areas of life. If a pair of other roles in which he has excelled were added, their number would equal the four Emmy and eight Grammy awards he received by the time the new facility of Spelman College was the focus of a topping-out ceremony.

A long-standing building tradition is to "top out" a new structure with a tree at its highest point to honor the donors, architects, contractors, builders, and other people involved in its construction. On the Spelman campus an evergreen tree was placed at the highest point of the Camille Olivia Hanks Cosby Center in September 1994.

For groundbreaking ceremonies three years earlier, Dr. Camille wore a special hard hat. Her brief remarks emphasized the importance of honoring "African-blooded sisters of the past, the present, and the future." Sporting a soft Spelman hat with upturned brim, on the same occasion Dr. Bill said that the building is "our gift to the world and in turn, that's what every graduate of Spelman will be—a gift to the world." Whatever the color of a person's skin and regardless of one's background, Dr. William Henry Cosby Jr. is living proof that barriers topple when excellence and ability are wedded to laughter.

W. E. B. Du Bois is treated in chapter 5.

12
Edwin L. Drake

Seneca Oil Suddenly Gushed Past the Medicine Cabinet

Describing the region then called Allegany, a 1795 gazetteer noted that it had long belonged to the Seneca Indians. Three prominent chieftains were known to white men as Cornplanter, Half Town, and Great Tree.

"In Allegany," J. Scott wrote, "is Oil creek: It flows from a spring much noted for a bitumen resembling Barbadoes tar, and is known by the name of Seneca Oil." If he knew that bitumen was familiar to the ancients, the author failed to say so.

This viscous stuff was put to use by a young Hebrew woman who daubed it on a vessel she wove of bulrushes to make it waterproof. Bitumen used by his mother saved the life of the baby Moses.

More than five thousand years ago the black substance, now called pitch or asphalt, oozed from wells and pits that became celebrated because of it. The ancients valued it for caulking rafts and boats used on the Euphrates River. When it was found to be a mortar suitable for holding sun-dried bricks together, it began to be shipped in bulk for great distances.

At spots not far from the Allegheny River, bitumen collected around the mouths of springs. Oil that seeped from bitumen-producing rocks was rare and mysterious. These qualities made it so greatly prized as a home remedy that members of the general public in the British colonies never had enough Seneca oil to use it casually.

S. M. Kier, whose business was operated on Pittsburgh's Canal Basin, sold at both wholesale and retail. He called his oil,

69

"a natural remedy possessing wonderful Curative Powers."
According to labels on bottles, the oil cured diseases of the
chest, windpipe, and lungs. It was all but magical in its effect
upon diarrhea, cholera, piles, rheumatism, gout, asthma, bron-
chitis, and scrofula. In addition, claimed Kier, there was no
better remedy for burns, scalds, neuralgia, tetter, ringworm,
blotches, and pimples on the face, deafness, chronic sore eyes,
and erysipelas.

A scholar more or less skilled in classical languages scorned
the old name and insisted that the oil coming from the rocks
should properly be called petroleum. Kier adopted it, but few
ordinary persons used that word until an unexpected chain of
events made rock oil abundant and cheap.

SEVEN YEARS before the outbreak of the Civil War, a group of spec-
ulators in New York became interested in Pennsylvania's unique
product. Calling themselves investors, they formed the Pennsylvania Rock Oil Company and put together about five thousand
dollars to operate it. Since every household medicine cabinet
in the Northeast held a bottle or two of Seneca oil, an increase in
production could mean substantial profits.

Soon they bought a big spring, earlier swapped by an owner
for a cow, that was locally noted for the Seneca oil that collected
on its surface. Nearby was the small settlement of Titusville,
home to about 150 people. During more than three years, nothing took place to boost the value of the land held by the Pennsylvania Rock Oil Company. The discouraged owners gave up
their quest and leased their holdings to a quick-dollar seeker.

Edwin L. Drake, a drifter for much of his early life, is known
to have worked as a hotel clerk and as a clerk in a general store.
For a time he may have poled barges along one of Pennsylvania's canals. Having become a railroad conductor and bestowed
upon himself the honorary title of colonel, he found financial
backing and began boring a hole into the ground near Titusville.

No one knows what Drake hoped to find when he began
work late in 1857. There are strong indications that he expected
to discover a lode of salt somewhere in the vicinity of the
spring noted for at least seventy years as a source of Seneca oil.

Colonel Drake, working with a single assistant, attempted
for four months to bore through clay and quicksand. His dis-
couragement vanished when he heard that nine barrels of

Edwin Drake's Titusville well.
[DRAKE MEMORIAL MUSEUM]

Seneca oil had been purchased in New York. Produced at Tarentum—a region named for the tar that was found there—the shipment brought $275.19 from the Kerosene Oil Company.

Having devised an improved drilling technique, Drake continued his efforts for week after week. On August 27, 1859, nearly nineteen months after work was started, his drill bit penetrated bedrock. Soon a mixture of oil and water came to the surface when a pump was started.

Investors and businessmen in adjoining states quickly learned that Pennsylvania and Drake had given the nation a new source of illuminating oil and lubricant for machinery. With oil from sperm whales already in short supply and the price of candles rising rapidly, the first petroleum well was believed to be a sure source of wealth.

Soon dozens of other wells were in production. So many of them clustered in the vicinity of the Drake discovery that a seventeen-mile stream took the name of Oil Creek. Seldom more than three feet deep but sometimes nearly one hundred feet wide, it flowed into the Allegheny River at a point that became known as Oil City. Wagons and flatboats began taking

*Early experiments
with petroleum
almost cost the life of
William S. Rosecrans.
[J. C. BUTTRE
ENGRAVING]*

oil to Pittsburgh, and railroad executives discussed the possibility of building a line to Oil City.

By September 1861 some who operated in Pennsylvania's
petroleum fields no longer had to depend upon pumps. Several
flowing wells, each of which yielded as much as three thousand
barrels a day, had gone into production. This enormous increase
in the volume of oil, coupled with near hysteria about an esca-
lating Civil War, knocked the bottom out of petroleum prices.

When a forty-two-gallon barrel of crude oil that had been
transported to New York brought only ten cents, numerous
wells were abandoned. Since it was not worth shipping to
market, large quantities of oil were allowed to run into Oil
Creek. Slowly drifting down a series of rivers, some of it eventually reached the ocean. No one protested this earliest of oil
spills; environmental concern was far in the future.

Other troubles were of much greater interest. An 1859 fire at
the Rouse well on Oil Creek left eleven workers dead and
twenty others badly burned, making national headlines. Indi-
vidual tragedies were not uncommon. Having turned to oil
from coal, William S. Rosecrans found partners and built a
refinery. During a laboratory experiment, fire nearly ended the

life of the man destined soon to become a major general and to lead armies fighting for the preservation of the Union.

Wartime prices fluctuated wildly. From the low point of 10¢ per barrel during the fall of 1861, petroleum jumped to more than $7.00 in 1864. Fast-increasing exportation to foreign markets helped stabilize the industry. Yet the value of the substance no longer known as Seneca oil varied between 49¢ and $1.87 per barrel in 1862.

A few farsighted leaders realized that to be profitable a petroleum company should own not only the wells but also the refineries and railroad tank cars. Again Pennsylvania led the way when Joseph N. Pew formed the Sun Oil Company in 1886. With Pennzoil already a major corporation, William W. Mellon formed the Gulf Oil Company in 1907.

Paradoxically, it was a man from outside the Keystone State who made its "rock oil" a truly huge industry. John D. Rockefeller of New York and Ohio was in 1865 a director of Benango County's Weikel Run and McElhinny Oil Company. His organization of the Standard Oil Company in 1870 led to a near monopoly in the United States and to wealth that made Andrew Carnegie's fortune seem small.

From Pennsylvania, oil fever spread westward until it peaked in Texas and Oklahoma. At the height of production launched by Drake's tiny well, no one could know that the United States would eventually become a primary purchaser of foreign oil.

Andrew Carnegie's rise from bobbin boy to philanthropist is summarized in chapter 4.

13
Herman Haupt
War Saw Transportation Take Giant Steps Forward

General McDowell, I hope you will go to the Potomac Creek in the next few days. It now has a bridge over which loaded trains are running; and I tell you that there is nothing on that bridge except beanpoles and cornstalks!"

Although admittedly weary with the burden of wartime responsibilities, Abraham Lincoln was clearly amazed. He spoke, of course, with the exaggeration that marks many of his humorous anecdotes.

Two Wisconsin regiments supplied 120 men, some of whom were experienced lumberjacks. Working around the clock, they hastily threw up a substitute for a bridge burned by Confederates. Rising fully eighty feet from the creek bed, a four-hundred-foot span was supported by three rows of trestles. Beams and boards needed for this enterprise were cut by hand from nearby trees. When finished, the structure elicited admiration from everyone who saw it.

Euphoria was short lived, however, when Confederate Gen. Stonewall Jackson soon cut the railroad that led to it. The "beanpole bridge" made famous by the president was for many months a vivid but useless symbol. U.S. Secretary of War Edwin M. Stanton, himself long connected with the Illinois Central Railroad, had been indirectly responsible for its erection.

WHEN STANTON took office on January 15, 1862, he moved swiftly to create the U.S. Military Railroad. A former superin-

Haupt's "beanpole bridge" was built in nine days by men with no experience in such work. [BRADY STUDIO, NATIONAL ARCHIVES]

tendent of the Pennsylvania Railroad, Daniel C. McCallum, was chosen to direct the new organization.

Just ninety days later Philadelphia native Herman Haupt was given charge of all construction and transportation on military railroads within the Union. He came with mixed feelings, for acceptance of the post meant he had to abandon a project upon which he had worked long and hard—the Hoosac tunnel.

For years Massachusetts had badly needed an extension of the Troy and Greenfield Railroad. Haupt had left the Pennsylvania Railroad in 1856 to build it, knowing that the Hoosac tunnel would be very difficult to construct. Criticism from officials of the Boston and Albany Railroad halted work on the tunnel after Haupt had spent his own and a great deal of borrowed money upon it.

Hoping to finish the job and to recover his personal investment, the engineer needed to keep in contact with Gov. James A. Andrew of Massachusetts. Hence he refused to accept a commission as a brigadier general and worked as a civilian volunteer without pay.

ALTHOUGH THE beanpole bridge made Haupt famous among men who fought in blue, the man himself counted the achievement as

Although he wore a general's uniform, Haupt never accepted a commission and worked without pay. [BRADY STUDIO, LIBRARY OF CONGRESS]

insignificant. He devised a new way to send messages, tripling the speed with which information reached Washington. Locomotives without cars behind them were sent into vital areas, transporting telegraphers with pocket instruments. Since lines usually ran alongside railroad tracks, operators could climb trees and quickly report on troop movements and other vital matters.

Known to subordinates as a born inventor, the native of Philadelphia's Germantown suburb had gone to England in 1857. Members of the Royal Polytechnic Society of Cornwall invited him there so they could learn about improvements he had developed for pneumatic drills.

Within a few months after joining the Union war effort, Haupt devised a radical new approach to bridge-building. At supply depots far from Confederate lines, workmen assembled quantities of structures they called "shad bellies." Sixty feet long, these devices were easily hauled by rail to sites where bridges had been burned but abutments were still standing.

Veteran fishermen had no difficulty in perceiving how Haupt's novel bridge segments came to be called shad bellies. [U.S. ARMY MILITARY HISTORY INSTITUTE]

Named for their resemblance to the stomach of a fish, they required only a few hours to be put in place. Thus Haupt was among the first to build prefabricated industrial structures.

Using interchangeable parts, artisans trained by Haupt rebuilt burned bridges throughout the war zone. Many went up so rapidly that Confederates began calling the man behind this engineering triumph "Mr. Magician."

That name seemed especially appropriate to Maj. Gen. William Tecumseh Sherman as his forces were moving into Georgia, pursuing the Confederate Army of Tennessee. Haupt's workmen rebuilt a 600-foot bridge over the Etowah River in less than six days. Later they completed a 90-foot-high, 780-foot bridge over the Chattahoochee River by noon of the fifth day of construction.

Having an urgent need to inspect some structures that could be seen only from the water, Haupt designed and built special pontoon rafts. After using these craft for a time, he designed a raft unlike any ever seen before.

Edwin M. Stanton was responsible for creation of the U.S. Military Railroad system. [U.S. SIGNAL CORPS]

Heavy timbers fastened two barges together, then a railroad track was laid from one end of the novel craft to the other. Haupt, who didn't bother to name his invention, rolled eight boxcars on to it. Moved rapidly by water, at their destination the loaded cars were pulled up on tracks that extended to the water's edge.

Decades later *Smithsonian* magazine listed the now-familiar land-sea cargo container as one of the ten most significant inventions of modern times. Because it could move from big trucks to oceangoing ships and vice versa, this device revolutionized long-distance shipping and is still used today.

Although less important for the future, another of Haupt's innovations helped turn the tide of the war. He devised a novel bridge with two levels of travel—one for the railroad and the other for wagons and soldiers on the march. Just sixteen feet high, this lattice-box structure featured prefabricated inter-changeable parts.

Having improved transportation greatly in a matter of months, Haupt returned to civilian life where his time and energy proved less fruitful than did his wartime efforts. He devoted all his energies to the completion of the Hoosac tunnel and then tried to collect the money owed to him. After years of effort, he had to accept a settlement that gave him only eight cents for each dollar he claimed as his due.

14
Elisha Kane

Nearly Anyone Can Win a Fight with a Polar Winter

Capt. Scott F. O'Grady of the U.S. Air Force became a national hero at 6:42 A.M. on June 8, 1995. That's when the pilot, code-named Basher 62, stepped from hiding and raced aboard a rescue helicopter. Shot down above northwestern Bosnia six days earlier, he was described as having survived against incredible odds; his diet consisting largely of insects and grass.

O'Grady received special training in survival techniques and used them skillfully in the rainy Bosnian forest. There is no record that he or his rescuers knew that a sickly physician from Pennsylvania played a major role in launching a chain of events that saved his life.

Decades earlier, Americans were astonished by news from never-before-explored regions near the North Pole. Elisha Kent Kane, like O'Grady a military officer, had spent eighteen incredible months in the frozen north before walking out, hale and hearty.

Queried by astonished reporters, the thirty-five-year-old from Philadelphia summarized his ordeal in a few words. "Until now, no one believed it possible to live on an Eskimo diet," he said. "I put my mind upon survival, ate blubber, and soon became accustomed to it. Nearly anyone can win a fight with a polar winter!"

That point of view was brand-new at the midpoint of the nineteenth century. Until Kane survived, it was taken

Elisha Kent Kane as depicted in an engraving made from a Brady photograph. [DICTIONARY OF AMERICAN PORTRAITS]

for granted that a nonnative could not survive in the frozen northland.

KANE DID not become that special kind of hero by choice. The son of an attorney, Elisha was reared in comfort spiced with challenge. Family tradition stressed that relatives had helped to establish America's earliest school of engineering, the Rensselaer Polytechnic Institute.

Elisha's father, a member of the American Philosophical Society, encouraged the boy to read *Robinson Crusoe* and *Moby Dick*. At age twenty-two he received a degree in medicine from the University of Pennsylvania. Fellow students confessed that they were a bit awed by their friend who didn't hesitate to say that he expected to live at a fast pace. His heart having been damaged by a long bout with rheumatic fever, he knew he had no years to waste.

Soon after the young man's graduation, his father persuaded the U.S. secretary of the navy to give his son a chance at the adventurous life for which he longed. As a result, the young doctor joined the U.S. Navy as an assistant surgeon. Aboard the USS *Brandywine* he went to China and to Africa before being sent to Mexico as a special messenger when war broke out between the United States and Mexico.

After delivering oral instructions from President James Polk to Gen. Winfield Scott, he spent five months in enemy territory. Sometimes he lay on his bed for many hours, unable to move. "What of it?" he asked concerned acquaintances. "I could live another six months or a year—or I could be struck down in half an hour."

Although never involved in a major military clash, he received a minor wound before coming down with typhus. Back home, half a hundred leading citizens of Philadelphia presented him with a sword, a token of admiration for his courage, they said.

Kane had asked to be assigned to the navy yard at Philadelphia for a time. Instead of remaining at home to rest and recuperate, he soon found himself aboard the ship *Supply*, scheduled to go to Portugal and then to Brazil. During the long voyage, he learned that shipping magnate Henry Grinnell was financing an expedition to the Arctic.

Sir John Franklin, a pioneer explorer of the region, had been missing since 1845. Hoping that he was still alive, in 1850 Grinnell persuaded the U.S. Navy to put together a search-and-rescue mission.

By the time men led by Lt. Edwin J. DeHaven were ready to sail, Kane had joined their ranks as senior medical officer. His account of the expedition and its abridgement as *Adrift in the Arctic Ice Pack* is considered a classic in its field.

No member of the Franklin party was found, but the physician insisted searchers had not gone far enough. Much evidence suggested that beyond Smith Sound there could be open water, he pointed out. Somewhere on the shores of such a body, Franklin or some of his men might be waiting to be rescued.

Grinnell donated the brig *Advance* for use in a second expedition. Backed by the secretary of the navy, John P. Kennedy, the project caught the public's imagination. Popular subscriptions provided ample funds for a new enterprise, this time led by Kane.

THE APPROACH of the polar winter found the Kane expedition on the shore of a previously unexplored body of water. In honor of the Philadelphia institution, it was named Rensselaer Bay.

In the Arctic, matters progressed from bad to worse. Scurvy broke out among the rescuers, and their sled dogs sickened and died. Two members of the party died and were buried in solid ice.

Kane later admitted having been frequently exhausted and occasionally frightened, but he never quit fighting. He knew that natives of the frozen north remained healthy on a diet of seal and walrus, so he decided to live like them. Soon he began to enjoy raw meat and praised it in terms no other explorer had ever used:

> The liver of a walrus (awuktanuk), eaten with little slices of fat, is a delicious morsel. Fire would ruin the pithy expression of vitality that belongs to its uncooked juices. This pachyderm is the very best fuel a man can swallow.

He realized that his appetite for raw walrus liver was a product of his determination to survive. He not only lived, but the new diet prevented his developing scurvy. Some of his men, however, refused to follow his example of trying to live like an Eskimo. They rebelled at the prospect of spending a second winter in the polar region. Reluctantly assenting to their demands, the man with a weak body that housed a will of iron led them to safety.

His eighty-three-day journey over the Arctic ice was hailed as "a retreat that was a masterpiece of victory in defeat." Defeat stemmed from the failure to find any trace of the long-lost Franklin party. Kane's two-volume account of his *Arctic Explorations* was a sensational success. Less than a year after it began to be seen on almost every parlor table in America, its author died at the age of thirty-seven.

Kane's shining legacy to the world was his demonstration that ordinary people could survive under extraordinary conditions. This later persuaded fellow Pennsylvanian Robert E. Peary to search for and find the North Pole. Richard Byrd and other pioneer explorers of the Antarctic acknowledged their debt to Kane. Modern-day survivalists such as O'Grady owe their lives to having followed the trail blazed by a near invalid whose name they may not know.

15
Mason and Dixon's Line

From a Philadelphia Base, the South Became Dixie

Penn's Land abounds with wild creatures such as I never saw in Devonshire. Many are said to be harmless, but some are considered dangerous. I try to keep my distance from a two-legged creature whose pungent odor sets the nose to twitching from a distance of half a mile."

That description of a Pennsylvania frontiersman is far more familiar in England than in America. Attributed to astronomer Charles Mason, it began making the rounds of British pubs about 1780 as a sure source of laughter.

Mason did not come to the New World expecting to settle here; neither was he, like Charles Dickens in a later period, an interested traveler in search of scenery and adventure. Along with his aide, Jeremiah Dixon, the astronomer had crossed the ocean as a skilled workman on assignment.

His job description was drawn up and a contract was signed in London on August 4, 1763. His employers were an unlikely lot—heirs to vast tracts of American land that had been a source of friction for eighty-two years. Frederick, Lord Baltimore, agreed with Thomas and Richard Penn that it was time to define the boundary between their holdings.

BOTH MARYLAND and Pennsylvania were founded as places of refuge for people enduring religious discrimination and persecution. In 1632 Charles I granted a huge, although unspecified, tract of land to George Calvert, first Lord Baltimore. The

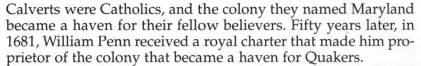

William Penn founded a colony but had only vague ideas about its borders.

Calverts were Catholics, and the colony they named Maryland became a haven for their fellow believers. Fifty years later, in 1681, William Penn received a royal charter that made him proprietor of the colony that became a haven for Quakers.

When the land was allotted, geographical knowledge of the regions was imprecise. Oceans, rivers, lakes, and mountain ranges were the chief lines of demarcation then employed in North America. Delaware Bay was a conspicuous example of such a natural boundary. Unfortunately, no east-west river was suitable to set Maryland apart from Pennsylvania. Almost one hundred years after the two colonies were launched, the proprietors agreed to settle the boundary dispute.

It was for this purpose that a skilled astronomer was employed. By observation of the stars, he could accurately determine locations from which to measure distances. Charles Mason, about thirty-three years old at the time he agreed to cross the Atlantic, had spent several years at the Royal Observatory in Greenwich, England. More than two hundred years later, global distances and time are still measured from this scientific center.

MASON REACHED Philadelphia with Jeremiah Dixon in November 1763. During a period of fifty-eight months, they tramped

Cecelius (George) Calvert, first
Lord Baltimore, received a vast
land grant but never saw it.

through the wilderness, forded rivers, observed animals and
birds, and kept their distance from frontiersmen when possible. Workmen under their direction permanently established
the Pennsylvania-Maryland boundary. In the process of doing
so, they also marked portions of the boundaries of Delaware
and of Virginia.

With the running of what today would be called a survey
line, neither the lords proprietor nor their surveyors could fore-
tell that the Mason-Dixon Line would later become symbolic of
division in American life.

To begin their work, the surveyors had to establish a starting
point. A house on Philadelphia's Cedar Street (later South
Street), then occupied by Joseph Plumstead, was found to be
the southernmost point in the city. When observations were
completed on December 30, boundary-makers were ready to
proceed with their work.

In making their measurements, the astronomers used 66-foot
surveyors' chains made up of one hundred links each. Short
distances were measured by use of wooden rods. Each rod was
16.5 feet in length, one-fourth as long as a chain. They seem to
have been equipped with levels so they could be held in true
horizontal positions.

The terrain was sometimes such that levels could not be used. In such instances, Mason and Dixon calculated corrections to be made for distances up or down slopes. Complex mathematical formulas were employed when measuring the width of rivers by what surveyors call "triangulation."

Ahead of those who tabulated distances, ax men cut a path through the forest. Cooks, tent keepers, chain carriers, and even a steward were included in the party whose number sometimes reached thirty-nine. Except for the visiting Englishmen, the party's personnel changed frequently. In some regions a majority of workmen were Native Americans. Two wagons filled with equipment were pulled by eight horses.

In England, workmen quarried stones and then prepared them for use along the Maryland-Pennsylvania border. The arms of the Penn family were inscribed on one side, and Lord Baltimore's arms were chiseled into the other side. Smaller stones, inscribed simply "P" and "M" were prepared for placement at each intermediate mile.

One of the five-mile markers put into place by Mason and Dixon. [THE ROYAL SOCIETY]

Vertical lines indicate measurements made to determine distances from the Greenwich observatory. [THE ROYAL SOCIETY]

From their starting point, Mason and Dixon extended a true horizontal line through swamps, over hills, and across rivers. During four years of work, they inched their way 244 miles westward from the Delaware River. Measured many years later with more complex tools, the boundary laid down by the Englishmen was found to be amazingly accurate.

All parties concerned accepted the work of Mason and Dixon. Decades later the line between Pennsylvania and Maryland was elevated into symbolic as well as geographical importance. Maryland refused to prohibit slavery within its borders, but Pennsylvania very early joined the ranks of so-called free states in which slavery was not tolerated.

Years later the former colonies that became states following the Revolution continued to have their boundaries defined by the Mason-Dixon Line. Influenced by the popularity of Daniel Emmett's 1859 song, "Dixie's Land," everything south of that line came to be known as Dixie.

16
Joseph Priestley
Persecuted, a Scientist Took Franklin's Advice

Walking briskly along a London street, the minister of a little church in Cheshire, England, held his head high. As he started toward the residence of Benjamin Franklin, sunlight glistened from the newly polished silver buckles of his shoes. These signaled that he was a member of the gentry; so did his cocked hat and powdered wig.

Joseph Priestley stopped swinging his cane as he mounted the steps before the door of the visiting American. He could hardly believe that his letter to the scientist, who was also a diplomat, had brought an invitation to talk with him about electricity.

Fourteen years earlier, Franklin had demonstrated the incredible. Lightning was produced by the same forces that caused feathers and bits of paper to cling to a ball of amber after it was rubbed.

Priestley would have considered it the high moment of his life simply to bow respectfully to the man who was noted for solving this puzzle of nature. According to the American, anything charged with electricity has two regions. Wrote the man from Philadelphia, "These remind me of the poles of the earth, so they should be universally designated as the (+) and (-) poles."

Today the son of a dyer and dresser of woolen cloth would not only bow to the great Franklin; two amateur scientists would converse about their experiments—perhaps for as long as half an hour.

Benjamin Franklin's famous lightning experiment captured the imaginations of several artists. Here he is cast as a modern Prometheus, bringing a different kind of fire to earth.

AFTER A warm greeting, Benjamin Franklin told his youthful visitor that they had more than one thing in common. Not only were both of them seeking to solve the mysteries of electricity, but both knew the meaning of poverty and had struggled to escape it.

Initially silent, Priestley nodded vigorous assent, then ventured to say: "If my notes are accurate, both of us also know that phlogiston is the elusive stuff that feeds fire . . ."

Far from guessing, the clergyman had read published reports by Franklin. He knew that they were in a minority among scientists; most chemists and physicists said there was no such thing as phlogiston. A factor as yet unknown, said most scientists, was required to support combustion. Many were hopeful that they might live long enough to hear of its discovery.

Franklin was proud to be a member of the American Philosophical Society, launched in Philadelphia in 1744. Yet he knew that Priestley's membership in the Royal Society carried even greater prestige. He gave his visitor hearty encouragement when Priestley said that he dared to hope he would soon publish a history of electricity.

"You may be close to making a great discovery of some sort," the American said as his visitor prepared to leave. "Come to Pennsylvania to pursue your experiments; you will find a most democratic and congenial atmosphere there."

Priestley, who didn't want to spend his ready cash on a transatlantic voyage, paused to make a confession. "I have been called a rebel against the king and the Anglican Church. That may lead me to act upon your invitation some day, but not for the present."

BORN AT Leeds in Yorkshire, Franklin's new friend was regionally noted for his skill in languages. He learned both Latin and Greek while attending a grammar school, then was tutored in Hebrew by a Congregational minister. French, Dutch, and Italian were studied without a teacher; so were Arabic and Syriac.

Fervently hoping to rise above his father's social and economic level, at the age of twenty-eight Priestley realized that to do so he must become a clergyman. No other vocation with prestige and a guaranteed living was open to him. For three years he studied at an academy described as "dissenting." Here teachers challenged—or dissented from—the structure and some of the doctrines of the established Church of England.

Ordained in 1762, Priestley obtained a parish in a rural village in Surrey. Many members of the congregation complained that he spent too much time trying to solve riddles of science, so he was shifted to Nantwich in Cheshire. It was from this small and financially weak church that he paid the first of several visits to Franklin.

Admitting to himself that he had failed in his chosen vocation, the son of a craftsman went to Warrington Academy as a tutor. He led students into the fields, where they reveled in finding fossils and collecting flowers. Believing himself to be under few restrictions, he lectured about electricity, astronomy, botany, and gasses—especially gasses that intrigued him.

A subsequent period of service as a minister in Leeds was followed by work as librarian to Lord Shelburne. From that post the man often regarded as a perpetual wanderer and rebel benefited from a jump in salary. As minister of the New Meeting in Birmingham, he began receiving more money than he had ever seen before.

From time to time Priestley served churches, taught youngsters, or compiled a catalog of books belonging to a nobleman. Regardless of how he earned his living, Priestley tried to spend a few hours every day in what he called his laboratory.

His freethinking religious views caused many ordinary folk to regard him with suspicion; that stance branded him as a troublemaker, they said. To them his sympathy for the French revolutionists was the last straw. A riotous mob set fire to his house, and in the blaze he lost his laboratory, his books, and many notes about his experiments.

DURING THE years since he had visited Franklin, Priestley frequently wished he had the necessary courage and capital to take the American's advice. When his beloved scientific equipment went up in flames, he scraped together enough money to leave England.

News that he was coming to America created a bit of a stir. A report about him was published in Philadelphia's *American Daily Advertiser,* and a few days later an editorial in this journal lauded the Englishman's scientific achievements.

He spent some time in Philadelphia, then went to live at Northumberland where his son had settled earlier. Soon Thomas Jefferson, who was beginning to plan the school that is now the University of Virginia, turned to Priestley for counsel about its course of study.

Even Jefferson did not then realize how many discoveries would eventually be credited to Priestley. Today the man who waited years to take the advice of Franklin is revered as a founder of modern chemistry. Some of his achievements rested upon accidents; most of them were far more important than he and his contemporaries realized.

Experimenting with a burning glass one day, he heated a number of substances. One of them, a compound of mercury, responded to "condensed rays of the sun" by giving off a gas "in which a candle burned with a remarkably vigorous flame." Wedded to the old phlogiston theory, he called the stuff "dephlogisticated air." Even when it became known as oxygen, he was not aware that he had found a substance that is basic to life on this planet.

Joseph Priestley's portrait was painted by Gilbert Stuart soon after the British parson came to Philadelphia.
[W. HOLL ENGRAVING]

"Pneumatic experiments" made over a period of many years did not end with the discovery of oxygen. Priestley also found ammonia and at least half a dozen other gasses. After having followed Franklin's example of turning his back upon his birthplace in favor of Pennsylvania, he discovered the killer gas we know as carbon monoxide.

To the average American, a stunning list of scientific accomplishments seems far removed from everyday life. Not so one of Priestley's other accomplishments. Describing what he had done with a gas and a fluid, the scientist said he succeeded in "impregnating water with fixed air."

A century later, that piece of work prompted the rise of dozens of global industries whose products are seen and used everywhere humans live. The substance first produced by Franklin's friend and by him called "impregnated air" is now familiar as carbonated water: soda pop.

Part Three
Keystone Curiosities

Daniel Boone eschewed his buckskins and moccasins for the occasion of this portrait, if he actually sat for the artist. [JAMES B. LONGACRE ENGRAVING]

17
Daniel Boone

Marvelous Tales Reached Harrisburg, London, and Paris

Many dark and sleepless nights have I been a companion for the owls, separated from the cheerful society of men, scorched by the Summer's sun, and pinched by the Winter's cold, an instrument ordained to settle the wilderness.

Some residents of Pennsylvania came across these lines before the United States was a decade old. No one bothered to describe their reactions, but a typical one must have been indifference.

In Great Britain and in Europe the response to "an account of the remarkable life of Daniel Boone" was quite different. Sophisticated citizens of London, Paris, Frankfurt, and other long-established cities were thrilled to learn that America's wilderness was being conquered.

Lord Byron later came across one of these early books that claimed to describe Boone's firsthand account of his struggle against Indians and nature. Thrilled by the image of Boone that was conveyed in just thirty-three pages, Byron praised the woodsman he never saw. When he devoted seven stanzas of his poem *Don Juan* to the man renowned for building Kentucky's first fort at Boonesborough, the adventurer became a permanent folk hero in Europe.

*John Filson of Chester County
is commemorated by
Louisville's Filson Club.*
[DICTIONARY OF AMERICAN
PORTRAITS]

Residents of Harrisburg and scores of other American towns probably didn't know that novelist James Fenimore Cooper was indebted to the earliest account of Boone's exploits. Years later, literary sleuths produced evidence that Cooper's famous Leatherstocking was modeled after the Boone of popular mythology.

BELIEVED TO have had no regular schooling, Daniel couldn't possibly have written about himself in the language that was used in the book *Kentucke*. The frontier hero was semiliterate at best and could barely scrawl a few misspelled words. There is no possibility that he could have talked about his adventures in the style attributed to him by author John Filson: "It was on the first of May, in the year, 1769, that I resigned my domestic happiness for a time, and left my family and peaceful habitation on the Yadkin river to wander through the wilderness in quest of Kentucke."

A native of Chester County, Filson elevated the Indian fighter into the ranks of American immortals. He spent time with

Boone somewhere in the West, almost certainly in Kentucky, and produced a 118-page volume that appeared in Wilmington, Delaware, eight years after the United States was formed. Much of the region described by Filson was then a county of Virginia, but about the time *Kentucke* was published, some of its residents had begun to dream of statehood.

Filson later helped to choose a spot on the Ohio River where he believed a town would thrive. Called Losantiville by him, it is today's Louisville. Here the Filson Club, still thriving, has gained national fame for its work in collecting and preserving regional lore.

No one knows why Filson chose to write about Boone rather than some other well-known frontiersman such as John James Audubon. Perhaps it was their mutual background in the Keystone State that drew together two men who had little else in common.

Ask any hundred persons stopped on the street to name the birthplace of Daniel Boone, and more than half will quickly answer with Kentucky. Most of the rest are likely to suggest North Carolina.

Novels and motion pictures in which Boone is a central figure seldom mention his first sixteen years in Pennsylvania. Born into a Quaker family, the sixth of eleven children, Daniel spent his boyhood on an isolated farm about halfway between Philadelphia and Harrisburg, nearly a day's walk from Reading. It was wholly natural for the boy to say "thee" and "thou" instead of "you" and sometimes to be teased by non-Quakers.

His prosperous blacksmith father kept a herd of cattle, so Daniel grew up in one of the handful of stone houses then standing in the region. A splendid house didn't mean a life of ease, however. He spent six summers with his mother and sister, separated from the rest of the family by four miles while he looked after cattle scattered over twenty-five acres of fine grassland.

It was during this period that at age twelve he received a rifle as a gift from his father and soon became locally renowned as a marksman. Earlier he had dug up a young tree, shaved its roots into a knob, and armed himself with what he called his "herdsman's club."

Some clues suggest that he became well acquainted with Indians during this period, for they were numerous in the

In everyday life, young Daniel Boone looked like the Indian fighter whose story was told by Filson.

Pennsylvania backcountry. Boone's father and other settlers whose parents had crossed the ocean to reach it considered the wilderness to be a wonderful place. Writing to relatives in England, one of them exulted, "In this country, you can shoot a deer, dress the hide, and wear pants from it a day after you directed the fire of your rifle toward it."

By 1750 when some of the older Boone children had left home, the Boones heard stories of rich land far to the south that could be had for almost nothing. With Daniel and five other children going along, they guided their wagons toward the Shenandoah Valley. From its southern tip they moved into the river drained by North Carolina's Yadkin River.

Most young males who accomplished such a journey were happy to settle down and rear their children as Tar Heels. Possibly influenced by Indian trader and adventurer John Finley, Daniel was a conspicuous exception to this rule. He wandered

The blockhouses and palisades of Boonesborough were not completed until years after Boone reached the site.

to Florida and came home praising that region, but his youthful bride refused to go there with him.

At age thirty-five, when a man was supposed to be settled down for life, he recruited a tiny band of followers and set out to cross the Allegheny Mountains. Passing through Cumberland Gap, they reached a wild frontier where they built a tiny fort, Boonesborough.

Measured by any standard, the subsequent life of the man from Pennsylvania was filled with adventures enough to fill several books. He spent a period as a captive of Indians, helped to organize Kentucky as a county of Virginia, and for years lived off the land—literally.

HAD DANIEL Boone spent his life in and around the region in which he was born, he might have become rich by the standards of the time. His decision to be a wandering adventurer meant a life of privation, danger, and hardship. It also elevated the native of Berks County into the role of the "first white man of the west."

That title, bestowed upon him in an 1847 biography by Timothy Flint, helped to complete the transformation of one among many hunters and Indian fighters into a lasting folk hero.

18
George M. Dallas

Without Honor in His Own State

Described as having "a decidedly patrician nose plus eyes that compelled attention," George M. Dallas was handsome—and he knew it. He reveled in Philadelphia's formal gatherings, at which he appeared wearing a coat of the very latest cut. As a member of a prosperous and highly regarded family, he entered the political arena naturally.

Before he filed for his first contest, Dallas had his eye upon Washington. If he was going to hold offices, he planned for them to become bigger and bigger.

No one was more keenly aware than Dallas that a series of obstacles stood in the way of his plans. Rivers and mountains divided Pennsylvania's million-plus citizens into five distinct regions. Each was largely self-centered, so it would be difficult for anyone to gain the support of three or more of them.

No other urban center in the state came close to being a rival of Philadelphia. In the entire nation, only New York exceeded it in size during the era destined to be dominated by Andrew Jackson of Tennessee. Although Harrisburg was the capital, fewer than five thousand people lived there. Pittsburgh's twenty thousand citizens could deliver only one-tenth the number of Philadelphia's votes. Lancaster, about one-third the size of Pittsburgh, constituted the only other city of any size.

A distinguished resident of Philadelphia with an impeccable background naturally held a strong advantage in the city where the United States was born. Outside Allegheny County, it was

George M. Dallas was among the most distinguished-looking politicians of his day.
[THOMAS B. WELCH ENGRAVING]

a different story. In most of the state's four other regions, James Buchanan had many devoted followers. This situation meant that Dallas could not avoid a long and bitter struggle with the man who also had his eye upon the White House.

After earning a diploma from Princeton, George studied law before becoming secretary to Albert Gallatin. His father, Alexander J. Dallas, then U.S. secretary of the treasury, had encouraged him to accept the position. "Gallatin has tremendous influence," he pointed out. "He is powerful in the state and in Washington; you can learn a great deal by observing him in action."

As a member of what today would be called the Young Republicans, George initially supported the presidential aspirations of John C. Calhoun of South Carolina. Soon, however, he concluded that the star of Andrew Jackson was ascending, and he decided to rise with him.

Experience in local offices made him an obvious candidate when there was a vacancy from Pennsylvania in the U.S. Senate. He was seated before the controversy between Calhoun

A glance at Andrew Jackson supports the view that "Old Hickory" was an appropriate nickname. [GEORGE M. BREUSTLE PORTRAIT]

and Jackson became a matter of major national concern. Led by the former vice president, South Carolina enacted legislation designed to make laws of the United States null and void. Jackson promptly threatened to send in troops to see that the laws were obeyed. Senator Dallas, by now a leader of the Democratic-Republican Party, never wavered in his support of the president.

Rewarded for his faithfulness by being named U.S. minister to Russia, he spent less than three years there before returning to politics at home. When Democrats met in Baltimore on May 27, 1844, to choose a candidate for the White House, some expected a quick decision. With Dallas a prominent member of the convention, veteran observers believed former president Martin Van Buren or Sen. Lewis Cass of Michigan would get the nod.

During seven ballots, neither leading candidate gained on the other. As a result, the delegates turned to James K. Polk of Tennessee. When he was chosen, the vice presidential nomination declined by Silas Wright went to Dallas. The Democrats won by a narrow margin on November 5, so for the first time a

*James K. Polk of Tennessee
accepted Dallas as his running
mate.* [LIBRARY OF CONGRESS]

native of Pennsylvania stood first in line to occupy the White House should the president fail to serve his full term.

Dallas knew that the traditional role of the vice president consisted largely of standing and waiting. Things were different in 1845, however, and long-simmering disputes were likely to erupt at any time in the Senate. With divisive issues pending, Dallas would preside over debate in the Senate and in so doing he would have to take a clear stand on those divisive issues.

Except for growing sectional strife over slavery, no national concern excited more interest than that of the tariff. High taxes upon imported goods hurt the agricultural states of the South but helped the industrial North.

President Polk then announced that the most important act of his administration would be a reduction of the tariff. He needed the support of his vice president and expected it.

After a lengthy study of the issue, Dallas decided that it was in the national interest to support Polk. By doing so, he realized that he would be unpopular at home. Miners and manufacturers

By 1852 the protective tariff was depicted as making the North (right) fat while the South (left) starved. [U.S. WEEKLY TELEGRAM]

of the Keystone State were ardent backers of "a wall of tariffs high enough to cut off or to reduce foreign competition."

When it became known that Dallas was working to win support for a reduction in tariffs, the voters of Pennsylvania were enraged. At the intersection of major streets in Philadelphia, a native son was hanged in effigy. Editors of the *Philadelphia North American* informed readers that Dallas had sold out to the slave owners of the Cotton Belt. Other newspapers denounced his stance as infamous and treacherous.

Feelings ran so high that the vice president warned his wife to be ready to leave home if her safety should be threatened. That did not happen, but he knew that he would never again hold high office in Pennsylvania.

After supporting another issue unpopular in the North—the admission of Texas as a state—Dallas left the political arena for good. Asked by President Franklin Pierce to serve as U.S. minister to Great Britain, he reluctantly accepted appointment to that post.

The *Dictionary of American Biography* later characterized the man from Philadelphia as a "gentleman in politics." That label, conferred after his death, would have been indignantly rejected by Pennsylvanians who never forgave him for having helped to lower the tariff. To many of them he remained "an assassin of Northern industry, a destroyer of the coal and iron industries."

Although reviled at home, the one-time mayor of Philadelphia was revered in a region far to the west. John Bryan had built a cabin at a crossing on the Trinity River in 1841. By the time the tariff issue reached the boiling point, a village had sprung up around Bryan's homestead.

When growth of the place enabled it to be chartered in 1856, a few residents remembered the man from the North who had helped to win statehood for Texas. As a result, the city of Dallas, Texas, commemorates the vice president whose political brawls are now all but forgotten.

Albert Gallatin's story appears in chapter 3; James Buchanan was involved with numerous other Pennsylvanians.

19
Harriet Lane

The Queen of Washington Society

Old Buck won't be much of an improvement over Pierce," grumbled William L. Marcy of New York.

"Not in looks," admitted Howell Cobb of Georgia. "But I've seen his niece, and I can tell you that she's a tidy bundle! Since he says he has no intention of taking a wife, I hope she will be the new mistress of the White House."

Marcy, outgoing U.S. secretary of state, knew that Cobb expected to become the new president's secretary of the treasury. Reluctantly preparing to leave Washington, the New Yorker turned to the burning topic of the day.

"Since you are a southerner, born and bred," he began hesitantly, "maybe you can tell me what Buchanan will do if South Carolina goes out."

"I have no idea," responded the Georgian. "This much I do know, though; he's been a congressman, a senator, and minister to both Russia and Great Britain. Don't be fooled by his habit of closing one eye when he talks with you. This tall fellow from Pennsylvania knows his way around. If he sees trouble coming, you can be dead sure he won't do anything to rock the boat."

Throughout the North and the South, everyone knew that the smashing Democratic victory in the election of 1856 came at a time of increasing tension. In the home state of "nullification" leader John C. Calhoun, rallies had been held in Charleston and Columbia. At them, thousands applauded

*James Buchanan,
Pennsylvania's only
president, was
committed to a
policy of no civil war.*
[BRADY STUDIO,
LIBRARY OF CONGRESS]

when speakers promised to lead South Carolina out of the Union if the new administration showed signs of reducing the power of states to chart their own courses. Viewed from any perspective, it was clear that the new president who hailed from Lancaster would face many hard decisions.

IT WAS easy for James Buchanan to settle the question of who would plan receptions, levees, and dinners. Years earlier, the only bachelor chief executive had adopted his orphaned nephew and niece. When President Franklin Pierce persuaded him to go to London as ambassador, Buchanan took Harriet Lane along and turned household affairs over to her. She was attractive and experienced; he was sure that no one could want a more fitting hostess for the White House.

As soon as the president's decision to use Harriet was made public, Washington society leaders glowed. With Jane Pierce as first lady, life in the capital had been dull and dreary. At age twenty-seven, Old Buck's rosy-cheeked niece looked eager to enjoy life and knowledgeable about how to do so. Rumor had

With Harriet Lane as hostess, festive parties and elaborate receptions were commonplace at the White House. [NATIONAL ARCHIVES]

it that Britain's Queen Victoria was so taken with the violet-eyed American that she urged her to marry a nobleman and stay in England.

Millionaire William W. Corcoran, whose mansion was within walking distance of the White House, approved when he learned that Harriet would be the new queen of Washington society. Having talked briefly with the auburn-haired beauty, he appraised her as "vivacious, keen-minded, and fully abreast of the times."

Corcoran was less enthusiastic about news that Harriet's first cousin, who was also Buchanan's ward, would serve as the president's private secretary. "He is young and inexperienced," said the financier destined to be commemorated by the Corcoran Art Gallery in Washington. "They call him 'Little Buck,' and that is as good a title for him as any; he is too young and inexperienced to look after matters of state."

Buck Henry, who seems to have performed better than many expected, was appalled when he learned that his uncle would

An East Room reception attracted hordes of dignitaries. [HARPER'S WEEKLY]

have to foot the bill for White House entertainment. Years later he reported that during many months, the cost of presidential parties often exceeded Buchanan's monthly salary of $2,083.33.

Harriet Lane was responsible for most of the overruns. Knowing her sixty-five-year-old uncle to be generous, Harriet seldom had to wheedle. Her smiles and dimples were enough to persuade him to go all-out to show that the United States was no longer a backwoods nation.

That was evident when the U.S. Revenue Service took unprecedented action. At a time when women were not generally honored, officials named their newest and finest cutter the USS *Harriet Lane*. This splendid six-hundred-ton side-wheel steamer was set aside for the use of "Baron Renfrow" when he paid a formal visit to Washington and stayed in the White House.

Actually Albert Edward, the nineteen-year-old Prince of Wales, the royal visitor was traveling incognito. He was puzzled by the president's wry neck that seemed to cause him to

The USS Harriet Lane *was equipped with both sails and a steam engine that drove the side wheels.* [U.S. NAVY]

cock his head to one side or the other. Buchanan vanished from his thoughts, however, when he boarded the *Harriet Lane* for a trip down the Potomac to Mount Vernon.

At George Washington's tomb, the prince took off his hat as a gesture of respect. He then planted a small tree and returned to Washington for an elaborate evening party. Planned by Harriet, the future king called the evening "a smashing success." Entertainment included the song "Listen to the Mocking Bird," composed in honor of Harriet.

A delegation of visiting Japanese dignitaries, the first to visit the United States, had been equally impressed a few months earlier. Their stay in the nation's capital triggered a giddy round of social events that caused another significant deficit for Buchanan's bank account.

THE ARRIVAL in Washington of the Republican president-elect and his wife early in 1860 signaled an end to an era that some had described as "four years of doing nothing." Buchanan consistently had refused to take actions that might lead to civil war, but his successor, Abraham Lincoln, had gone on record as ready to do whatever might be necessary to preserve the Union. Although his wife had grown up as a Kentucky belle, she very early made it clear that "the Lane years of expensive entertainments were over."

With the end of Harriet Lane's reign as queen of Washington society, the capital became even more bleak and austere than during the Pierce administration. With the nation divided and South Carolina having seceded in response to Lincoln's election, war was imminent.

When a small flotilla was sent to Fort Sumter to hold that site for the Union, the vessel named for James Buchanan's niece was among them. That mission failed, so the *Harriet Lane* returned to patrol duty on the Potomac River. In that role the Prince of Wales would not have regarded the vessel as suitable for a pleasure cruise.

Armed with two 32-pounder guns and a rifle whose barrel was eight inches in diameter, she was one of the first Union vessels to effect a capture of a Confederate vessel. After having taken the schooner *Iris* and its cargo of naval stores in May 1861, the former revenue cutter went on patrol duty.

Japanese dignitaries, the first ever to visit Washington, posed with their guards and their American hosts. [LIBRARY OF CONGRESS]

Under Capt. Thomas T. Craven, she helped to prevent the Southerners from shutting off capital-bound traffic on the Potomac River.

After taking part in a successful Federal assault whose target was Cape Hatteras, North Carolina, the *Harriet Lane* joined the Atlantic Blockading Fleet. Later operating against Confederate forces at Galveston, Texas, the vessel was captured. When her officers made a daring escape in April 1864, she again came under the command of the U.S. secretary of the navy.

The colorful and action-packed career of the USS *Harriet Lane* was an ideal postscript to the four years in which a Pennsylvanian's niece ruled Washington society.

20

Barbara Frietchie

Whittier's Instant Heroine Is Still Lauded

One of America's most famous poets was always looking for new and exciting subjects. Late in the summer of 1863 he was pleased to be visited by novelist Emma D. E. N. Southworth. Earlier she had said that she wanted to share a story with him, which she had heard directly from a person who was present at an unusually dramatic event.

Southworth told the poet that her tale revolved around a Quaker who was born in Lancaster County, Pennsylvania. During 1838–40 Whittier had lived in Philadelphia and edited an antislavery paper called the *Pennsylvania Freeman*. Thus he suggested he might have known the central figure of the still-unshared story.

Southworth shook her head. "You would have had to visit Frederick, Maryland, to meet Barbara Frietchie," she said. "She went there years ago and never came back to the place of her birth."

Pausing an instant, the novelist laughed, then said: "Dripping wet, she never weighed more than 110 pounds but she didn't have a dull bone in her body. When she was forty she married a glove maker who was just twenty-six years old. No sooner had they said their vows than she made her bridegroom change his name from Frietschie to Frietchie—don't ask me why."

"Interesting," agreed Whittier, "but an unlikely subject for a stirring poem."

John Greenleaf Whittier accepted a story of courage without trying to verify its authenticity. [DICTIONARY OF AMERICAN PORTRAITS]

Sparkling, his visitor condensed for him an episode that was widely circulating in Maryland. According to it, the northward advance of Robert E. Lee's Army of Northern Virginia caught many Federal leaders by surprise. One of Lee's most valuable subordinates, Stonewall Jackson, camped with his men just outside Fredericksburg in early September 1862.

On the following morning, the Confederate general rode through the town on West Frederick Street. Since he was at the head of a long column of soldiers, Jackson was the first man in gray to be seen by long-time resident Barbara Frietchie.

Probably dressed in plain Quaker gray, Frietchie snatched a small U.S. flag from her Bible and rushed to a window of her attic. There she waved the Stars and Stripes to taunt the Southerners.

A Confederate officer called out to her, "Granny, put that flag down and get out of the window before somebody shoots you!"

Ignoring the warning, the ninety-five-year-old woman stubbornly remained at her post, waving her little flag until the last Confederate filed through Fredericksburg.

WHILE LISTENING to the novelist's account, Whittier made some hasty notes. Within a few days he completed a rough draft of a dramatic poem. Dispatched to his editors and entitled simply

An artist's conception of the high moment depicted Frietchie defiantly waving her flag at the Confederates en route to Antietam. [LESLIE'S ILLUSTRATED]

"Barbara Frietchie," the sixty-line saga was published in the October 1863 issue of the *Atlantic Monthly* magazine.

According to the poem, forty Union flags were flying in Fredericksburg on the morning when an attack seemed imminent. The residents quickly hauled down these emblems, but Barbara Frietchie "bravest of all in Frederick-town," went upstairs with one of them.

Wearing a slouched hat in the poet's account, Jackson saw the flag and ordered some of his men to fire. They quickly obeyed, with results that could have been anticipated:

> . . . out blazed the rifle blast.
> It shivered the window, pane and sash:
> It rent the banner with seam and gash.
> Quick as it fell, from the broken staff
> Dame Barbara snatched the silken scarf.
> She leaned far out on the window-sill,
> And shook it forth with a royal will.
> "Shoot if you must, this old gray head,
> But spare your country's flag," she said.

Blushing with shame, the Confederate general signaled for his men to resume their journey. During four hours the tread of marching feet caused Frietchie's tiny cottage to tremble and quiver, but her bullet-torn flag fluttered defiantly until all the Southerners were gone.

Published when weary Northerners were reading repeated accounts of Union defeats, "Barbara Frietchie" became immensely popular. Issues of the magazine in which it appeared had hardly reached readers before the poem's central figure was hailed as a national heroine.

Considerably later, scholars who examined records learned that Jackson did not pass through Frederick on the day in question. Inspiring as was the poem about a brave old woman, the event it memorialized could not be substantiated.

Once doubt was cast upon the Frietchie story, someone came up with a modification. According to this version, men in blue rather than men in gray were passing through the town on the way to Gettysburg. Barbara Frietchie really did wave the Stars and Stripes with enthusiasm, it is said, but the objects of her zeal were men who had sworn to die for the Union if necessary.

Maj. Gen. Jesse Reno, says the modified account, was intrigued at the sight of a very old woman showing her patriotism. Hence he persuaded Frietchie to sell to him the tiny flag that she waved so vigorously and so long.

Researchers have also failed to turn up any evidence supporting the Reno version of the story. Within a decade of the war's end, military and civilian authorities alike agreed that the story relayed to Whittier in Massachusetts was without foundation.

When he began hearing rumors that his "Barbara Frietchie" was being questioned, the poet indulged in a rare display of anger.

> I had no reason to doubt its accuracy then [at the time it was written], and I am still constrained to believe that it had foundation in fact. I have no pride of authorship that would cause me to waver from my fidelity to the truth.

Whittier might have saved the time and effort it took him to pen this statement of support for the Frietchie story as he heard it. The general public was not greatly interested in finding that the poem was accurate. They simply copied it, memorized it, and recited it throughout the land with an enthusiasm that seemed never to wane.

Widespread admiration for the poetic but fictional account of a real woman's deeds failed to die. As a result, the patriot whose Quaker heritage didn't completely quench her fire became an instant heroine. Barbara Frietchie is still lauded for her courage in the face of the enemy.

21

George G. Meade

For Want of a Scribe, an Epic Was Lost

Meade is coming!" yelled a tall fellow who had scurried to the top of the reviewing stand. Before he resumed his seat, many spectators who had come for a once-in-a-lifetime event stood and saluted or held their hands over their hearts.

"Gettysburg! Gettysburg!" cried one of them. Scores of Pennsylvanians then joined their voices to produce a roar that could be heard for many blocks: "Gettysburg! Meade! Gettysburg! Meade!" they shouted over and over.

Leading eighty thousand veterans in blue, Maj. Gen. George G. Meade turned his head only once. When he saw that Andrew Johnson was not in the stand, he faced straight ahead and resumed his march. After the Army of the Potomac passed in review, he made his way to a spot reserved for him close to both the president and Lt. Gen. U. S. Grant.

May 23, 1865, was a day no one present would ever forget; for Meade, it was the high-water mark of his career. Only during this Grand Review commemorating the battle of Gettysburg did the victorious general receive overwhelming public adulation.

IN MANY respects the lack of widespread appreciation for his military leadership was Meade's fault. Aides insisted that his nickname of "Old Snapping Turtle" was appropriate. He had a blazing temper, they agreed.

Born in Cadiz, Spain, while his father was working as a naval agent, he seemed destined to have an affluent boyhood. Things

Triumphant Federal officers led thousands of troops through the streets of Washington during the Grand Review of May 1865. [HARPER'S WEEKLY]

changed quickly when the Spanish government refused to pay the bills submitted by Richard Meade. Impoverished, the family returned to Philadelphia and was supported by the wealthy grandfather for whom George was named.

Since he could get a free education at West Point, he chose that route, won an artillery commission, and fought briefly in the Seminole War. Meade then decided to become a civilian construction engineer, but his intermittent career in this field came to an abrupt halt at the age of forty-six.

Gov. Andrew G. Curtin of Pennsylvania, eager to supply the troops needed by Washington, persuaded Meade to accept a commission as a brigadier general of volunteers. Since the nation's capital was believed to be a military target, he was assigned to the defenses of the city. When the fort whose construction he directed was completed, he named it Fort Pennsylvania.

Ordered to lead troops into battle, Meade was unscathed at Mechanicsville and Gaines's Mill, but took two wounds simultaneously at Glendale, Virginia. One bullet struck just above his hip and clipped his liver before passing out close to his spine. His arm was mangled by the other projectile seconds later.

After a period of recuperation in Philadelphia, he rejoined his men but never fully recovered from that June 30, 1862, battle of White Oak Swamp. Recurrent bouts of severe pain from his wounds probably contributed to Meade's proverbially bad temper. Still, he fought bravely and successfully at Antietam, Second Bull Run, and Chancellorsville.

News that Lee seemed to be launching an invasion of Pennsylvania was followed by orders to move rapidly to the north. Near Fredericksburg, Maryland, Meade was abruptly awakened at 3 A.M. on Sunday, June 28, 1863. An orderly then handed him a message just received from Washington. He scanned it hastily, stared blankly in disbelief, and blurted that this was something he had not sought and did not want.

From the U.S. War Department, General in Chief Henry W. Halleck ordered him:

> You will receive with this the order of the President placing you in command of the Army of the Potomac. You will not be hampered by minute instructions from headquarters. Your army is free to act as you may deem proper under circumstances as they arise.

NO COMMANDER of a Union army had been given a free hand earlier; Lincoln made many decisions that today would be rendered by joint chiefs of staff. Ignorance of Confederate plans was one reason Meade was told to do what he considered right. Lee and his generals were known to be advancing through Maryland.

A major victory by Lee could lead to diplomatic recognition of the Confederate States of America, so it was imperative to stop the Army of Northern Virginia. No one in Washington knew where the men in gray planned to strike.

Meade took his orders literally. In an unprecedented series of instant promotions, he elevated three captains to the rank of brigadier general. Aware that Governor Curtin had called for one hundred thousand volunteers to serve for one hundred days to protect their state, Meade moved cautiously toward the Maryland-Pennsylvania border.

Very early on July 1 he received a report that the Confederates had burned the military barracks at Carlisle. His cavalry having been ordered to find where enemy forces were concentrated, he soon learned that a struggle was under way at Gettysburg. Meade did not reach the site of the mammoth battle until it was joined. Having been thrust into command, he directed Union forces for more than two days.

After the war, scores of books began to appear about the struggle at Gettysburg, perceived by many as the turning point of the Civil War. Lee was as honored and revered in the North as he was in the South. Nearly every general who had been present at Gettysburg was lauded in a lengthy tome.

Incredibly from today's perspective, the victor at Gettysburg was all but overlooked. No significant biography of Meade was published until 1897, when it was brought out by the Philadelphia house of H. T. Coates and Company. This despite the fact that Meade was one of a handful of wartime leaders who received the formal Thanks of Congress.

WHY WAS so little said about the exploits of the man born in Spain and reared in the city of Benjamin Franklin? His sudden elevation in rank, immediately followed by the most crucial victory of the Civil War, was the stuff of which epic sagas are made. Glowing action-packed accounts of Meade's accomplishments did not reach the general public because every experienced writer who traveled with the Army of the Potomac joined in a conspiracy of silence.

Numerous military commanders, notably Maj. Gen. William Tecumseh Sherman, made a public show of despising correspondents and reporters. Sherman, however, learned to cooperate secretly with them in order to use them for his own ends. Meade never gave the slightest hint that he wanted the goodwill of writers and had no desire for them to publicize his actions.

After Gettysburg, Meade's mistreatment of a reporter for the *Philadelphia Inquirer* became legendary. Having written a story that the general did not like, Edward Crapsey was placed under arrest and thrown in the guardhouse for a night. The following day, the camp's soldiers were formed into long lines. Guards hung a cardboard notice around Crapsey's neck that labeled him a "Libeler of the Press," and the unfortunate journalist was

Gen. George G. Meade often looked as though he really was an "Old Snapping Turtle." [LESLIE'S ILLUSTRATED]

forced to trudge the length of the parade ground to the tune of "The Rogue's March." After this punishment, Crapsey was expelled from the camp.

The humiliated journalist easily persuaded his fellow writers to avoid mentioning Meade's name in their dispatches. When it was impossible to avoid referring to him, they agreed to confine their notice of his actions to as few sentences as possible. Thus Meade's wife soon received a letter in which the general told her, "I find the paper barely mentions the Pennsylvania reserves, and my name never appears."

With professional writers united in an informal conspiracy that was seldom violated, during the final crucial months of the conflict the general public heard little or nothing about the man who saved the Union at Gettysburg. The silence was so pervasive that it has prevailed for almost 150 years. Having no scribe to write his epic story, Meade still has received only a fraction of the acclaim given to many whose accomplishments fell far short of his.

22

Louisa May Alcott

Woman of the Family During an Era of Male Breadwinners

Forty ambulances full of rebels wounded at Fredericksburg are here; hurry up, you're wanted!'

"'What shall we have to do?'

" 'Wash, dress, feed, warm, and nurse them for the next three months, I dare say. Now you will begin to see hospital life in earnest. Come with me to the ballroom; the worst cases are already there.' "

That hurried exchange between a veteran nurse and a thirty-year-old newcomer took place during the last week of 1862. Nine months later James Redpath of Boston published Louisa May Alcott's 102-page volume of *Hospital Sketches*, written in third-person style.

Following her brief conversation with an older woman, the author described her feelings:

I am free to confess that I had a realizing sense of the fact that my hospital bed was not a bed of roses just then, or the prospect before me one of unmingled rapture.

My three days' experience had begun with a death, and, owing to the defalcation of another nurse, a somewhat abrupt plunge into the superintendence of a ward containing forty beds. There I spent my shining hours washing faces, serving rations, giving medicine, and sitting in a very hard chair.

Pneumonia was on one side, diphtheria on the other, with five typhoids plus a dozen dilapidated patriots, hopping, lying, lounging about, all staring more or less at the new "nuss."

She suffered untold agonies, but concealed them under as matronly an aspect as a spinster could assume.

Life in the Union Hotel Hospital had little in common with Louisa's earlier years. Situated in Georgetown and adjacent to the nation's capital, the institution had been converted from a commercial hotel. Government-built facilities were incapable of accommodating the hordes of sick and wounded men who were being sent to Washington in increasing numbers.

After three weeks the volunteer nurse developed "a sharp pain in the side, cough, fever, and dizzyness." Diagnosed as having developed "typhoid pneumonia," she was treated with huge doses of calomel that made her weaker than ever. Soon she became delirious and had to return home. Meanwhile, letters written to her family had been saved with no idea that they would be converted into a book.

BY THE time she was eight, Louisa had decided to become a writer. After keeping a journal for a time, she wrote a poem

Carver Hospital in Washington. Note the unusual pattern of the stars in the flag hanging from the ceiling. [U.S. SIGNAL CORPS]

called "To a Robin" and soon afterward began delving into books from her father's shelves. *Flower Fables*, a novel produced at age sixteen, was eventually published but brought the aspiring author no royalties.

She was ecstatic when *Gleason's Pictorial* paid five dollars for a story in 1851. During the following year a story used by the *Boston Saturday Gazette* brought her ten dollars, so she began writing in every hour not devoted to family duties. Scolded by her distinguished father for wasting her time "scribbling foolish stories," she persisted. Probably encouraged by Nathaniel Hawthorne and Ralph Waldo Emerson, in 1860 her writings began to appear occasionally in the *Atlantic Monthly*. The magazine's standard payment of fifty dollars per story, to say nothing of the publication's long-standing prestige, meant a great deal. Suddenly the dark-eyed young woman with rosy cheeks was elevated a trifle in her father's esteem.

VERY EARLY, the girl born in Germantown shared in family pride that her father, Bronson Alcott, was a distinguished educator. According to him, the failure of Pennsylvania Quakers to afford him a living necessitated a move to Massachusetts. Changing addresses more frequently than was then common, he and his family alternated for a time between Concord and Boston.

Louisa and her sisters did not know that Ralph Waldo Emerson extended financial aid to their father. Louisa and Anna were captivated by him, however, and even little May smiled and held up her arms when the famous man entered their home. Awed by the passion displayed by abolitionist John Brown, they were also enthralled by Henry David Thoreau.

The gray trousers and straw hat worn by the man who made Walden Pond famous were in sharp contrast with the appearance of Bronson Alcott. Usually impeccably dressed in black, he presented an imposing appearance even after his coattails began to be a bit shiny.

Eventually his daughters came to expect that any school operated by their father would fail. He could discourse about philosophy for hours with learned friends, but he never managed to provide adequately for his family. Alcott was so immersed in classical literature that he reacted casually to word that a sudden storm had hit his all-important barley crop. Louisa, her sisters, their mother, and a boy from the neighborhood raced into the field with sheets and managed to save much of the grain.

After Louisa's letters from the hospital were published in modified form, her father briefly left his beloved books. He stayed away from them only long enough to find that his daughter's stories, taken to a publisher, evoked no interest. Back home, he reported that the man with whom he talked suggested that Louisa might try to write a novel for girls.

TWO MONTHS after beginning work upon a thinly disguised story in which the members of her family were central, Louisa had settled upon a title—*Little Women*. Anyone acquainted with Bronson Alcott's poverty-stricken family had no difficulty in discovering the real identity of Meg, Jo, Beth, and Amy.

Shortly after the novel's publication, letters poured in begging the author to write more and to let Jo marry the central male character, Laurie. "No," Louisa usually replied, "the facts in the story are true and cannot be altered." As a result, Jo continued to be a successful and unmarried career woman through many printings of Louisa's novel.

With 1870 just around the corner, publishers of the first edition dispatched a royalty check. When it arrived, every member of the Alcott household crowded around to gape and to gasp. During decades in which Bronson Alcott had studied and taught, no year had seen him bring in earnings anywhere close to Louisa's eighty-five hundred dollars.

THE SMASHING success achieved by the author of *Little Women* soon brought radical changes in the lives of every member of her family. Clearly, Louisa had assumed the role then normally played by a father and husband. Each member of the family and everyone who knew them were aware that the novelist was now the breadwinner. Yet little if anything was said in disparagement of Bronson Alcott.

No child of the teacher whose learning was coupled with financial failure now had to observe a limit of two meals a day. Soon the Alcott residence, suffering from years of neglect, was repaired and refurbished. Debts incurred by Bronson were repaid as rapidly as possible, despite the fact that some were many years old.

The success of her writing made Louisa May Alcott the family breadwinner. [Concord, Massachusetts, Free Public Library]

May, who had cherished what seemed to be futile dreams about studying art, could now go to the school of her choice. Eventually her older sister provided money that enabled her to spend months in Europe, where she became a friend of Mary Cassatt.

Widespread interest in *Little Women* persuaded magazine editors to pay the author increasingly large fees for short fiction. Their publication did not prevent her from completing other books. Although less successful than her first novel, some of them boosted her royalties significantly. Having stepped into the place her father would normally have occupied, Louisa wanted him to have every possible comfort.

Colossal as her growing income seemed to Bronson, he did not dream that one day his daughter's novel would be translated into dozens of languages. Long after readers began eagerly to devour it, the first of several motion picture versions of *Little Women* went into theaters of the nation.

Almost invariably using the label "distinguished" when she mentioned her father, Louisa was distraught when he died on

March 6, 1888. She was buried beside him only three days after his funeral.

Some who knew the family intimately believed that Louisa died of grief at having lost the only man she truly loved. Despite the fact that her life was much shorter than that of her father, this verdict is suspect; she may have suffered from any of half a dozen fatal illnesses.

About one aspect of the life of the enthusiast who lasted only three months as a volunteer nurse there is no debate. Louisa May Alcott remains alive and well as vivacious Jo March, the pioneer career woman who is the immortal central character of *Little Women*.

The story of Mary Cassatt is told in chapter 2.

23
George Washington

A Fighter in and out of Pennsylvania

We got it launch'd & on board of it & set off; before we got half over we expected every moment our raft would sink & we perish.

Notwithstanding all our efforts we could not get the raft to either shoar, but wer oblig'd, as we were pretty near an island, to quit our raft & wade to it.

The irregular schooling of George Washington, age twenty-one, had ended six years earlier. On his second military expedition, made on behalf of Virginia, he reached Fort Le Boeuf after a perilous river crossing. Now the site of Waterford, its garrison refused to obey his 1753 demand that they leave the place instantly. Washington was disappointed but not surprised. His long journey into Pennsylvania was made because French soldiers and their Indian allies were numerous there.

Soon, warned colonial leaders, these troublemakers were likely to launch all-out war against settlers as well as British soldiers and officials. Lt. Gov. Robert Dinwiddie was among those who feared the French. Trying to limit their power, some of his men threw up fortifications where the Allegheny and Monongahela Rivers meet to form the Ohio River, site of present-day Pittsburgh.

When enemies seized the tiny installation, Washington withdrew southeastward. At Great Meadows he directed the hasty building of tiny Fort Necessity and near it defeated a French body led by Coulon de Jumonville. This action launched the ten-year struggle known as the French and Indian War. Pitting soldiers from two European nations—England and France—the struggle was destined to decide control of the largely unexplored American West.

Fort Necessity was held by British forces for only a few weeks. Three months after surrendering it to a vastly superior force, Washington agreed to become an aide-de-camp to newly arrived Gen. Edward Braddock. Soon a new expedition against Fort Duquesne, at the origin of the Ohio River, was under way.

Illness delayed Washington's third foray into Pennsylvania. He managed, however, to join Braddock's forces on July 8, 1755. One day later, British and colonial troops marched into an ambush in which their English general was killed.

Without having formal authority to do so, the young Washington took charge of the survivors. Two horses were shot from under him, but he managed to rally his frightened men and to lead many of them back to Virginia.

This exploit brought the twenty-three-year-old soldier without formal military training a coveted commission as colonel in command of colonial forces in Virginia. As a result, he spent the following three years trying to make the frontier strong enough to withstand raiding parties. Serving under Gen. John Forbes, he helped to build Fort Pitt on or near the site of Fort Duquesne after the French had abandoned it.

In September 1774 he was back in Pennsylvania as a member of the First Continental Congress. Some of the delegates who assembled in Philadelphia looked askance at the fellow who took his seat wearing his Fairfax County militia uniform. If Washington noticed, he paid no attention; he fought throughout the American Revolution with no change in appearance.

By the time the Second Continental Congress assembled in 1775, most colonial leaders considered war with Great Britain to be inevitable. Since they could not fight without a commander, they chose Washington as commander in chief of the Continental army. Before leaving Philadelphia he learned that four major generals and eight brigadiers would serve under him.

During a formal ceremony held on July 3 he took command of what foreign observers called "an undisciplined and untrained mob, whose members will run for home at the first sound of gunfire."

When Washington took command of the Continental army, his men were not nearly so disciplined as depicted here. [HARPER'S WEEKLY]

Small by comparison with the British troops under Gen. Sir William Howe, the Continental forces failed miserably in their attempt to hold New York City. Fighting a delaying action against impossible odds, the colonials withdrew through New Jersey into Pennsylvania. Many men grumbled at the prospect of again facing the British; their enlistments would expire on December 31, 1776, and they were more eager to go home than any foreign observer knew.

Surveying a seemingly impossible situation from his head-quarters not far west of the Delaware River, Washington devised a daring plan. From his Pennsylvania base he launched an attack on Christmas night.

Most Americans know the thrilling story of his surprise victory over the hired Hessian soldiers who were quartered in Trenton, New Jersey. *Washington Crossing the Delaware*, a painting by Emanuel Leutze, is well known. Not so well known is

Winter quarters at Valley Forge enlarged the legend of Washington, who stayed with his troops and endured their deprivations.

the fact that, contrary to the artist's interpretation, the colonials crossed the river from their Pennsylvania base in pitch darkness. Instead of the comparatively elegant craft depicted by Leutze, Washington and his men used Pennsylvania-built oar boats designed by Robert Durham. Clumsy but capable of bearing immense loads, Durham boats were about eight feet wide. Their length varied from about forty to about sixty feet, so in addition to many soldiers these craft were sturdy enough to take eighteen cannon across the river. Without Durham boats, Washington would hardly have dared to attack a strong force of hardened veterans. After the American victory was won, many men who had been preparing to take off their uniforms decided to reenlist.

Along with Congress, the lawmaking bodies of the colonies were stingy with money and supplies. Scarcities contributed largely to the loss of Philadelphia and the subsequent withdrawal of the Continental force to winter quarters. Conditions at Valley Forge were so miserable that the name of the Pennsylvania site has come to be a synonym for a place of great hardship.

*Gilbert Stuart's 1795
portrait of Washington is
probably the best known
other than that which
appears on the dollar bill.*
[H. B. HALL ENGRAVING]

Five years later their victorious commander in chief paid a
formal farewell to his officers before returning his commission
to Congress. To him and to them, it appeared that George Washington's military leadership in Pennsylvania had come to an end.

They were wrong, however. In 1794, the sixty-two-year-old
Washington, president of the United States, raised troops and led
them toward a region west of the Allegheny Mountains. By far the
most serious of early civil disturbances in the United States, the
Whiskey Rebellion was quashed without bloodshed. Had Washington not personally taken the lead in plans to put down the rebellion against the new central government, the United States might
have experienced secession before it was a decade old.

Virginians in the Tidewater region where George Washington was born rightfully claim him as a son of the Old Domin-
ion. Yet from start to finish, the Pennsylvania military career of
the man revered as the "father of his country" spanned more
than two generations. Were his exploits within the borders of
the Keystone State stricken from the record, the story of American independence would not be what it is.

*Gilbert Stuart of Philadelphia painted portraits of many
prominent people; his painting of Washington is still widely
reproduced.*

Part Four

Off the Beaten Path

Susan B. Anthony at about age thirty.

24
Susan B. Anthony

America's Second
Declaration of Independence

Holding documents in their hands, five women edged
toward the speaker's platform. Few spectators eagerly waiting
for the July Fourth observances to begin paid more than passing attention to them. In the mood of excitement that prevailed
at the Centennial Exposition of 1876, it was comparatively easy
for a person to go to an unassigned place without being called
to a halt by a military guard.

Holding herself stiffly erect, Susan B. Anthony led the way.
Other factors aside, it was appropriate that she should serve as
the official standard-bearer. Born into a Quaker family, she was
in a congenial atmosphere in Philadelphia. Also, as state law
prohibited a married woman from making a contract, Anthony
had signed the papers renting "fine, large parlors in a desirable
part of the city" at 1431 Chestnut Street. There on May 25 the
National Woman Suffrage Association opened its headquarters. Rent was paid from five-dollar gifts made by fifty-two
members, fifty-one of whom had husbands and so could not
enter into a contract in Pennsylvania.

Officers of the association sent from their new headquarters
a formal request to officials of the Centennial. "Women of
America respectfully desire five minutes during the celebration of the one hundredth anniversary of the Declaration of
Independence," they wrote. Almost as an afterthought, they

The main building of the Centennial Exposition of 1876 was a masterpiece of glass and metal.

pointed out that women were known to have purchased more than one hundred thousand dollars of stock issued to help defray the Centennial expenses.

Gen. Joseph R. Hawley, president of the Centennial Commission, politely but firmly notified them that the schedule was full and could not be altered. Since President U. S. Grant would be represented by the acting vice president, he was approached by the ladies. Thomas W. Ferry warmly assured them that he sympathized with their demands that women be given political rights, but he had no authority to yield the platform to them.

Ferry, Hawley, and other officials knew they would be busy looking after the wants of visitors from afar. Dom Pedro, emperor of Brazil, would have a seat of honor. So would Prince Oscar of Sweden, in spite of the fact that he was just sixteen years old.

Plans called for recognition of Count Rochambeau of France in the audience, along with officials from Prussia, Russia, Turkey, Japan, Australia, and numerous other countries. By the time a few speeches were made and these men from afar were applauded, the audience would be weary. There simply was no time for a woman to address the mass of celebrants.

ONCE THEIR polite request was rejected, Susan B. Anthony went into action. From her brother, publisher of a newspaper, she secured an admission ticket that identified her as a reporter. Four colleagues also managed to persuade relatives or friends to name them as members of the press. With these tickets in hand, Susan Anthony, Matilda Gage, Sara Spencer, Lillie Blake, and Phoebe Couzins made their way to the press box. Situated near the platform, it constituted an all-male segment of the audience until these "reporters" took their seats.

Members of the Woman Suffrage Association had come to terms with reality. They were reconciled to the fact that it would be impossible for one of them to read their recently drafted Declaration of Women's Rights. They dared to hope, however, that they would find an opportunity to distribute printed copies.

RICHARD HENRY LEE of Virginia stepped to the podium to read in thrilling fashion the Declaration of Independence adopted in Philadelphia a century earlier. When he bowed at the end of the reading, thunderous applause almost drowned out the lively Brazilian national anthem that was played as a tribute to Dom Pedro.

Tossing a slight smile that partly concealed her grim face, Anthony took advantage of the noise and bustle. Deftly making her way to the platform, she offered a copy of the daring new "Woman Declaration" to Ferry. He turned pale, shook his head vigorously, and gestured for guards to remove her.

Before they could reach her, Anthony mounted the steps and took center stage. She quickly read a few sentences, then thrust a printed copy of the complete document into Ferry's hand before he knew what she was doing.

"When their declaration thus became a part of the day's proceedings," one observer wrote, "the ladies turned, scattering printed copies as they passed down the aisle. On every side eager hands were stretched; men stood on seats and asked for them while General Hawley shouted, 'Order! Order!'"

Alexander Graham Bell exhibited his telephone at the 1876 Exposition, but few visitors responded enthusiastically to it. [NEW YORK TRIBUNE]

FOR SIX months, more than eight million people paid the fifty-cent admission fee to experience the Centennial Exposition. They gaped at the mammoth Corliss engine and agreed that the main building really was the largest man-made structure in the world. In the hall of sculpture, some were especially moved by *The Dying Indian Chief* but many felt that the work of art they would never forget was *The Freed Slave.*

Comparatively few people paused to take a quick look at the original *Mason and Dixon Journal,* especially purchased from Nova Scotia for the exhibition. Tens of thousands, however, listened to the songs of Philadelphia native Stephen Foster, and many purchased the sheet music.

George Washington's false teeth were on display, along with the arm and hand of an uncompleted statue by a French artist. Soon it would go to New York to be affixed to the Statue of Liberty. A machine that stood six feet high but had no identifying label attracted considerable interest, yet relatively few visitors were excited by Alexander Graham Bell's demonstration of his telephone.

A few pieces of embroidery from the hand of Queen Victoria were admired. Relatively few persons were awed by a walk through Libby Prison, however. Dismantled in Richmond and reassembled, this building was once crammed with Union officers, prisoners of the Confederacy. Old Abe, the aging eagle who had survived the Civil War as mascot of a Wisconsin regiment, was by far the most popular exhibit in the Military Hall.

J. H. RAPER of Manchester, England, expressed a verdict shared by thousands who were present at America's birthday celebration. "The grandest moment of July 4, 1876, came when suffragettes outwitted dignitaries," he said.

"If this young nation celebrates another centennial of its independence, it will be adorned by portraits of five determined women. Thanks to them and their followers, women will by then be treated as first-class citizens."

Stephen Foster's story appears in chapter 27, and the work of Charles Mason and Jeremiah Dixon is described in chapter 15.

25
Allegheny Arsenal
A Pittsburgh Tragedy

The American public was stunned and horrified by the 1995 bombing of the federal building in Oklahoma City that killed 169 people. When an 1862 explosion in what is now metropolitan Pittsburgh claimed 80 lives, hardly anyone outside the immediate area paused to mourn or rage.

For residents of the borough of Lawrenceville, Wednesday, September 17, began as an ordinary day. Hundreds of workers filed into the Allegheny Arsenal. Operated by the U.S. Army, unlike some arsenals that served chiefly as storage depots, Allegheny was a major manufacturing plant. Parrott guns that could hurl 10- and 12-pound projectiles were made there in limited numbers. A few heavier guns constructed elsewhere were stored there as well. More important for the local economy and the Union war effort, .54- and .71-caliber cartridges were prepared at the armory. This activity made the arsenal the largest employer of the region. Job-hunting country girls came from miles around and found employment there.

When a cartridge was test fired, it emitted a brief "cracking noise" that could sometimes be heard across the river in Pittsburgh. Around 2 P.M. on the fateful day, 125,000 of these small voices united to produce a mighty roar that was heard for miles.

In Washington, Brig. Gen. James W. Ripley soon received a terse report. According to the post commander, John Symington, nearly 200 people were at work in the arsenal when the tragedy occurred. Of these he said that at least 150 were women and that young boys made up most of the remainder. "Civil

144

All U.S. arsenals used young women and boys as cartridge fillers. Following the practice of the day, they were paid by the piece rather than with hourly wages.
[LIBRARY OF CONGRESS]

authorities of Lawrenceville and Pittsburgh will launch an investigation at once," he promised.

As described by a reporter for the *Pittsburgh Daily Post,* three separate blasts came so close together that many mistook them for a single explosion. As was the case 133 years later in Oklahoma City, buildings surrounding the site of the blast were also damaged. One such structure was a Presbyterian church "some distance from grounds of what many residents have come casually to label 'the Park.'"

EARLIER, THE Allegheny Arsenal had figured in official military documents and local news. Ardent Unionists accused U.S. Secretary of War John B. Floyd of trying to ship Pennsylvania-made arms to Southern states that were threatening to secede. A telegram to President James Buchanan touched off a high-level inquiry.

Pittsburghers William Wilkins, William F. Johnston, W. Robinson, Thomas Williams, and Charles Shaler exposed the deal. On December 25, 1860, they charged:

An order has issued from the War Department to transfer all the effective munitions of war from the arsenal in this city to Southern forts. Great excitement has been created; we advise that the order be immediately countermanded. If this is not done we cannot be answerable for the consequences.

Had this news come from the arsenal at Harpers Ferry or Saint Louis, the president would have taken it seriously. Since it was issued from his own state, Buchanan, who was preparing to yield the White House to Abraham Lincoln, was so alarmed that he did not sleep. Floyd resigned, aware that he would be forced out of office if he tried to retain it.

Nine days after Buchanan heard of the plan to move munitions from Allegheny to the South, high-ranking officials joined in the clamor surrounding the scandal. One of them was Simon Cameron of Pennsylvania, who eventually succeeded Floyd. He wrote that "the removal of cannon from the Allegheny Arsenal" must be taken very seriously.

Possibly as a result of Cameron's concern, Congress began asking questions. Official Washington was greatly relieved by another telegram from Pittsburgh on January 4, 1861. This time, Mayor George Wilson and the president of the city's common council expressed "much pleasure" that the orders to ship weapons from the Allegheny Arsenal had been countermanded.

SOON THE weapons center was again in the news. Lt. Gen. Winfield Scott ordered Symington to ship to Carlisle Barracks "500 complete sets of cavalry equipments: saddles, bridles, saddle-bags, and blankets." These were quickly dispatched to Maj. George H. Thomas, commander of cavalry at the post north of Harrisburg.

Gov. Oliver P. Morton of Indiana and Gov. Richard Yates of Illinois did not fare so well; both wanted heavy guns from Pittsburgh for the defense of their states. Symington regretted that none were available; he had just taken eighteen 24-pounder

*Simon Cameron succeeded
John B. Floyd as secretary of
war and was subordinate only
to the president.* [NICOLAY
AND HAY, ABRAHAM
LINCOLN]

and eighteen 32-pounder guns from storage and sent them to
Maj. Gen. John C. Frémont.

ALTHOUGH BARE of cannon, the Allegheny Arsenal was of vital
national importance. Eight of its fourteen "apartments," as they
were called, made up a "laboratory" in which more than 175
youthful cartridge-fillers labored. In the main building that
faced Butler Street, 300 others spent their days preparing paper
shells and other essentials.

Since Wednesday was payday, there were few absentees and
"some fifty of the hands in the laboratory" had pocketed their
wages before the blast. Like scores of boys who worked in
Washington and at other sites, these cartridge-fillers were paid
by the piece rather than by the hour or day. As a result, most of
them were at the bottom of the pay scale and received less than
one dollar per day.

At Allegheny and every other arsenal, employees had been
nstructed concerning safety precautions. At quitting time in
the late afternoon, finished cartridges were removed from the
laboratory to prevent the possibility of a disaster. Workers who

unloaded barrels of gunpowder were told to lose as little as possible and always to clean up after a spill.

These rudimentary safety regulations may have been ignored. It is equally possible, though, that a shell being prepared for shipment may have been dropped. The explosion of a shell or the firing of loose gunpowder from a spark made by metal wheels rolling over granite cobblestones probably sent much of the Allegheny Arsenal skyward.

Survivors gasped out tales of horror. One girl sent "flying through the air" was seen to break into fragments. An arm landed close to a wall while a foot sailed to the gate. "A piece of skull was found a hundred yards away, and pieces of intestines were scattered about the grounds."

Numerous victims, so badly mangled they could not be identified, were packed into plain black coffins provided by the government. Allegheny Cemetery donated a large lot, and burial ceremonies were held one day after the blast. Those who attended the mass funeral said they would never be able to forget the image of "thirty-nine coffins side by side, filled by those whom no one could recognize."

While mourners gathered in the cemetery, workers began to clear the site. A newspaper report said that for many yards around the center of the explosion "the ground was strewn with fragments of charred wood, torn clothing, balls [mostly of the minié variety, used in muskets], caps [used to detonate cartridges], grape shot, exploded shells, shoes, fragments of dinner baskets, steel springs from hoop skirts, cartridge paper, sheet iron, melted lead, &c."

The investigation by a coroner's jury revealed that the blast shook buildings along the Monongahela River as far away as Port Perry. Witnesses reported that ordinary friction matches were sometimes seen lying on tables and benches. One or two persons who had worked in the now-demolished laboratory believed that it was destroyed by an act of Confederate sabotage. Others admitted that near the points where barrels were handled, loose powder on stones was sometimes half an inch thick.

No conclusion was reached concerning the cause of the explosion, and to jurors it seemed futile to estimate the monetary damage. Those who died were given as decent a burial as circumstances permitted, Symington was replaced as post commander by Maj. Robert H. K. Whitely, and the Pittsburgh region tried to resume reasonably normal ways.

FEW FINANCIAL contributions or expressions of sympathy came from the people outside the vicinity of Pittsburgh. There were no mass meetings in distant cities at which citizens voiced angry protest at the needless deaths of youthful federal employees. A handful of newspapers far from Pennsylvania gave passing attention to the explosion at Allegheny Arsenal, but the majority ignored it.

Reporting from the U.S. Ordnance Office nearly a year later, Ripley insisted that "records of the office show no telegraphic dispatches between December 20 and 30, 1860, inclusive, to Major Symington or other person in Pittsburgh or at the Allegheny Arsenal." Unfounded stories were behind indignation that Floyd was shipping big guns from Allegheny to his native South.

The deaths of about eighty young women and boys—perhaps more—were treated far more casually than were false rumors. Outside the area surrounding the arsenal, both the North and the South were absorbed with other events.

At Sharpsburg, Maryland, armies in blue and in gray came together early on the morning of the great explosion. By sunset it was clear that September 17 would be remembered as the bloodiest day in American history. News that at least twenty-five thousand casualties were suffered during the battle of Antietam overwhelmed the nation. Because of the day on which it occurred, the Pittsburgh tragedy received little attention—then or now.

James Buchanan is central to chapter 19, and the story of John C. Frémont may be found in chapter 28.

26
Corbin and Pitcher

Molly Sure Rammed a Mean Sponge

Members of the Executive Council of Pennsylvania took an extraordinary step on June 29, 1779. They granted to a woman the sum of thirty dollars "for her immediate necessities" and referred an account of her needs to the Continental Congress.

Delegates who made up the larger colonial body did not dally. On June 6 they voted to relieve the distress of Margaret Corbin. Under the terms of the legislative act, a woman born in present-day Franklin County was granted a military pension—something no other American woman had received.

The lawmakers decreed that "during her natural life or the continuance of her disability" the former Margaret Cochran would receive "one-half of the monthly pay drawn by a soldier." Pensions, tiny by today's standard, normally went only to veterans who were seriously wounded while fighting against the British.

After she married Virginia-born John Corbin and took his name, Molly followed her husband when he enlisted in Proctor's Pennsylvania Artillery. An expert matross, or cannoneer, he taught her the complex sequence of movements essential to firing a big gun. Just before inserting a charge it was necessary to ram the barrel with a sponge attached to a long pole. Only after having been properly cleaned in this way was a gun ready to deliver another blast.

George Washington's forces were thrown against the British at several points in the colony of New York. After a serious defeat on Long Island, the general decided to blockade the

Hudson River by holding Fort Washington, despite his knowledge that enemy artillery forces were decidedly stronger than his.

On November 15, 1776, soldiers sent to America by George III launched a furious cannonade against the patriots. John Corbin is believed to have been a member of a crew whose two guns were stationed at the north end of their fort. Corbin fought furiously until hit by a projectile. His widow then seized the pole he dropped and proceeded to sponge the cannon.

When the British overran the fort, they found Molly lying beside the cannon. Hit by three grapeshot, she had a mangled arm and a badly damaged breast. Despite her wounds, she somehow survived a bruising journey to Philadelphia in a wagon built not far from the city. When she began to recover her strength, she was released as her captors thought she would be of no value in an exchange of prisoners.

Tradition says that at war's end the Pennsylvania woman was made a member of an "invalid regiment" stationed in New York, all of whose members were crippled in battle. Corbin's widow is said to have insisted on being addressed as "Captain Molly." Although the title was not official, as part of her pension she demanded and received issues of rum that were regularly doled out to all veterans.

Molly celebrated all night on hearing of the adoption of the U.S. Constitution; this meant that a new nation had been created. She enjoyed only four years as a citizen of the United States, however, and at her death was buried near the West Point post to which she had gone about 1780.

MARY LUDWIG HASS, daughter of a German immigrant, grew up on her father's New Jersey farm just across the river from Pennsylvania. At about age fifteen she was sent by her family to Carlisle, where she became a servant in the household of Dr. William Irvine.

Domestic service for the physician lasted only a few months. Before her sixteenth birthday Mary became the bride of a Carlisle barber, John C. Hays. When Irvine gained command of the First Pennsylvania Regiment of Artillery, Hays enlisted and his wife went along as a camp follower. She remained with him after he transferred to the regiment in which John Corbin had served earlier.

Molly Pitcher stepped up to take the place of her husband at the battle of Monmouth. Her action brought her to the notice of Washington.

Cooking, washing clothes, and doing odd jobs for officers kept Hays's wife busy as his regiment moved from place to place. Crossing into New Jersey in 1778, it was soon stationed at Monmouth. British foes chose June 28, a particularly sweltering day, to stage an all-out attack against Washington's Continentals.

Soon after the battle began, Mary Hays found a spring of cold water and began racing back and forth from it with a pitcher of water. Some of the men who swallowed the precious liquid instantly started calling her "Molly Pitcher."

Some time during the heavy action of the day, Hays seems to have suffered a heat stroke. When he fell beside his cannon, Molly Pitcher is said to have taken over in his place. Just as Molly Corbin had done two years earlier, she demonstrated that she knew what to do around a piece of heavy artillery.

Tradition holds that Gen. Nathanael Greene, who saw Molly in action, personally led her to Washington so that the com-

Gen. Nathanael Greene reputedly took Pitcher to General Washington so he could personally commend her.

mander could thank her for the gallantry she demonstrated in battle. Before the American Revolution came to an end, members of many artillery batteries were using a colorful phrase that also entered popular speech. As a verbal tribute, "Molly sure rammed a mean sponge!" was applicable to both skirt-wearing cannoneers.

Military veteran Molly Pitcher settled in Carlisle, where she took a second husband and again found work as a servant. Forty-three years after Molly Corbin's career as a civilian volunteer was recognized, the General Assembly of the Commonwealth of Pennsylvania took notice of Molly Pitcher.

"For the relief of Molly McKolly," as she was by then known, lawmakers voted forty dollars on the spot and forty dollars annually for the rest of her life. Unlike Corbin, she never received a military pension from the nation whose freedom she helped to win.

PITCHER'S BATTLEFIELD heroism is not supported by a body of evidence such as that about Corbin's. Yet a tangled chain of circumstances made her the better known of the two. Much of her fame rests upon the work of artists who heard second- and third-hand accounts and reacted much like Whittier when he was told about Barbara Frietchie. They didn't bother to try to research the details; they simply commemorated Pitcher on canvas. Years later her statue in Carlisle became a major tourist attraction of the city.

Revered as the only known female cannoneers of the American Revolution, both Mollys were in financial straits after their wartime careers ended. Rewards given to them by grateful Pennsylvania lawmakers were tokens only, by today's standards. Yet they are remarkable because both were conferred during an era when it was taken for granted that only a male could be a veteran of service in an artillery battery.

27

Stephen Foster

America's Troubadour Never Saw the Suwannee River

Preservation of Florida's past is closely tied to the Stephen Foster State Folk Culture Center. Situated at White Springs on the Suwannee River, its name perpetuates the memory of a Pittsburgh native called "America's Troubadour."

Florida's choice of a riverfront site and a Pennsylvanian's name for its folk culture center is one of many tributes to Foster's lasting influence. When news of his death at age thirty-eight reached England, devotees throughout the island kingdom mourned. Editors of London's *Musical World* lamented that he would write no more of the songs that "during the last ten years were more successful than those of any other composer."

Born in Lawrenceville in 1826, Foster sang so sweetly about the nonexistent Swanee River that it gained a special kind of fame. Although the Suwannee River runs through Georgia and Florida, the composer never watched it flow and when he chose its name he deliberately altered its spelling.

At age fifteen the youngster living in what is now metropolitan Pittsburgh briefly attended a "college" where he studied music. Earlier he had taught himself to play the guitar and banjo and had already tried his hand at composing. Family members frowned upon a career in music, so at age twenty he was packed off to Cincinnati to keep books for his brother.

On formal occasions Stephen Foster, America's troubadour, dressed as a member of Philadelphia's society.

"Blackface songs," written in what passed for Negro dialect, were the rage of northern music halls. Foster soon tried his hand at composing for minstrels and began selling some of his works to Edwin P. Christy of New York.

Christy paid ten dollars per composition for all performing rights. At least twice he was in extraordinarily generous moods, so he paid the composer an extra five dollars for permission to attach his own name to Foster's work.

Stephen's brother Morrison, who later became his business manager, gave a detailed account of how one of Foster's best-known songs took shape. "One day in 1851 he came into my office and inquired, 'What's a good name of two syllables for a southern river?'"

He needed that name, he explained, for use in a new version of a song earlier made public under the title of "Old Folks at Home."

According to his brother, the composer was deliberately trying to break from his "Ethiopian" dialect and style. Yet for it to be useful on stage, he thought that his song must not focus on the Allegheny or the Ohio or the Delaware River. Nothing would do except a southern stream with a properly musical name, he explained.

Edwin P. Christy of New York made a small fortune from the songs for which he paid a pittance, including the rights to be credited as both composer and lyricist. [DICTIONARY OF AMERICAN PORTRAITS]

Cincinnati was probably as far south as the composer had ever gone. His "Old Kentucky Home" is traditionally linked with a prolonged visit to that state, but documentation supporting such an excursion is slim. A later one-time trip to New Orleans was his only substantiated personal encounter with the people and the land of the Deep South.

Morrison Foster suggested that Yazoo, a river in Mississippi, had a good musical sound. His brother rejected it since it had already been used in a popular song. Then Morrison pointed out that the Pee Dee flows through both North and South Carolina.

The composer's initial reaction was favorable, so he experimented with a song that would invite listeners to visit in imagination a spot "'Way down upon de Pee Dee River." Reflection persuaded him that the name, although unusual, wasn't quite right.

Looking through a pile of books near his desk, Morrison found an atlas and began searching for unusual, lyrical names of rivers. When he reached Florida and read "Suwannee," his brother was delighted. "That's it!" he reputedly shouted.

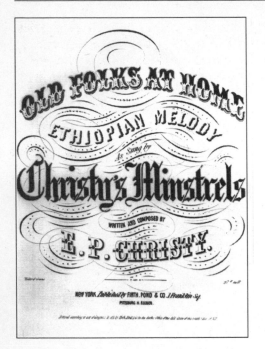

Title page of an early edition of Stephen Foster's "Old Folks at Home" that credited Christy with authorship. [NEW YORK PUBLIC LIBRARY]

According to Morrison, his brother cleared away part of the desktop. "On the spot Stephen wrote the name down," he said. "When the song was finished it began with a nostalgic emphasis upon a grand old region along the 'Swanee River.'"

With the name of the selected river slightly altered, Foster's new composition was approved by Christy. Entered for copyright on August 16, 1851, it was entitled "Old Folks at Home." According to the title page of sheet music, it was "An Ethiopian Melody, Written and Composed by E. P. Christy."

An instant hit in 1852, "Old Folks" was lauded as "one of the most successful songs that has ever appeared in any country. Publishers keep two presses running on it, and sometimes three; yet they cannot supply the demand." In a period when few songs achieved a lifetime sale of 5,000 copies, "Old Folks" sold 150,000 copies in two years. Soon it could be heard throughout England as well as the United States. Letters written by soldiers in the Crimean War said that the sentimental song by an American was one of two favorites among the fighting men.

Until the first copyright term expired in 1879, sheet music produced by Christy credited him with having written the words and composed the melody. After the initial printings, Foster was identified as having created the work, but these late printings had limited sales and brought him the only royalty payments he ever received from the song.

As a boy, Foster was familiar with Green Tree, Castle Shannon, Dormont, and Mount Lebanon. These and other place names of the Pittsburgh area were not used in his hit songs. Having only secondhand knowledge about the region that blackface entertainer Daniel Decatur Emmett called "Dixie's Land," Foster insisted upon singing about it.

At age thirty-two he spent a day or so in a rare activity. Drawing up a record of earnings from his published works, he tried to project his future income. "Old Folks" and all its arrangements went into the record as having yielded $1,647.46. He believed that with luck it might bring in another $100.

Stephen Collins Foster died January 13, 1864, in New York City. When his life and achievements were summarized for the *National Cyclopedia of American Biography,* he was described as having been "a penniless wanderer."

That characterization says a lot about the man who gave the world "Jeannie with the Light Brown Hair," "Oh! Susanna," and scores of other perennial favorites. During his final months in New York he is believed to have lived much like present-day street people.

A badly worn wallet found on his body held a few coins and a scrap of paper. It was inscribed, "Dear Friends and Gentle Hearts," believed to have been the working title of what he hoped would be a new hit song.

Foster's widow, who later became Mrs. Matthew Wiley, shared with his daughter about $132 in royalties from "Old Folks" during the first year after renewal of copyright. For decades it was nearly always listed among the ten best-loved American songs. Eventually the two women shared about $2,000 earned by the nostalgic lines about a river far away.

In the region drained by the Suwannee River, however, Foster's name is perpetuated by Florida's "living memorial." He is also commemorated by the Stephen C. Foster Georgia State Park on Jones Island, near the center of the Okefenokee Swamp.

*Stephen Foster's wallet,
empty except for a scrap of
paper and a few coins.* [NEW
YORK PUBLIC LIBRARY]

Nearly one thousand miles away, in the urban center to
which the troubadour never fully adjusted, New York University's Hall of Fame includes a bust of the northerner who sang
so tenderly about the South.

28
John C. Frémont

First Standard-bearer of the Republican Party

Shouts of "Order! Order!" were punctuated by banging of a gavel. When a degree of quiet was restored, the chairman of the national convention of the Republican Party put the purpose of the gathering into a single sentence.

"On the anniversary of the battle of Bunker Hill," he said, "you have gathered in order to give direction to a movement that will decide whether or not the people of our nation are to be hereafter and forever chained to the extension of human slavery."

Two years earlier, a handful of angry citizens came together in Ripon, Wisconsin. Congressional adoption of the Kansas-Nebraska Act of 1854 meant that there was a chance of establishing slavery in new western territories. Determined to change the course of the ship of state, Ripon citizens decided to base their campaign upon the views of Thomas Jefferson.

Adamantly opposed to the long-dominant Federalist Party, Jefferson labeled himself a Republican. He fervently hoped that aristocrats who dominated the Federalist Party might be forced to form a genuine republic. Such a political order would necessarily depend for its strength upon "the common man" instead of wealthy plantation owners, fur traders, and shipping magnates.

Once Jefferson was no longer a major political figure, many of his notions were discarded. Formation of a new Republican Party was seen as a way of involving ordinary folk while curtailing or even abolishing slavery.

Five months after ground was broken in Wisconsin, commissioners to a state convention in Jackson, Michigan, made the new name official. Delegates to other state conventions soon followed their example. As a result, from a grass-roots movement the Republican Party emerged as a national force.

Democrats had controlled the federal government for many years; if they could be overthrown, national policies would change. Simultaneously, a Republican victory at the presidential level would enable them to fill thousands of governmental posts.

To say that the political scene was fragmented is a gross understatement. Although slavery was the burning issue of the day, many people wanted to curtail the power of the federal government and strengthen that of the states. Because industry was largely concentrated in the North, that region generally favored a high protective tariff, which cost the South dearly.

Under the Federalist regime only about 6 percent of Americans were eligible to vote. Although the franchise had been gradually extended, it was still largely limited to twenty-one-year-old white males and older. Many states refused to permit an otherwise eligible male to register to vote until he had paid poll taxes or produced evidence of military service.

U.S. Secretary of War Jefferson Davis had defeated opponents in a recent contest over the route for a transcontinental railroad. Through his influence, it was scheduled to be built not far north of Mexico. Many denounced this decision as the result of political subterfuge and vowed to overturn it.

A prominent group called themselves Whigs, refusing to admit that they were perpetuating the doctrines of the old Federalists. Torn by conflicting loyalties and divisive issues, some of them—including Abraham Lincoln—moved into the new Republican Party.

Leaders of this movement turned their backs upon the time-honored system of choosing nominees by means of city, state, and regional caucuses. Although the concept of staging a national convention to select candidates was new, most Republicans favored it.

Therefore, on February 22, 1856, some of them came together in Pittsburgh. Their choice of date was not accidental; it reflected their hope that Washington's birthday would be a magnet that would attract unaffiliated voters.

The heads of Republican state committees in nine states who organized the Pittsburgh meeting were elated when representatives from twenty-three states arrived for discussions and planning. By far the most radical outgrowth of the Pittsburgh conclave was a decision to hold a national convention. Nominees for the posts of president and vice president of the United States would be selected when it convened in Philadelphia.

Democrats held their national convention in Cincinnati during the first week of June. To the disappointment of Stephen A. Douglas of Illinois, delegates chose Pennsylvania's James Buchanan on their seventeenth ballot to head their ticket. Long before they gathered in Philadelphia, Republicans knew that the native of Pennsylvania was the man they would have to beat.

At a February convention of the American Party, Millard Fillmore had been nominated. Widely called Know-Nothings because they tried to keep their aims and actions secret, this political organization wanted to exclude immigrants and Roman Catholics from office. Although strong in some states, the party was not regarded as likely to win the White House.

MANY OF the Republicans who gathered for their first national convention were confident of victory in November. William H. Seward of New York, who had expected to win the nomination very early, was viewed with doubt by delegates who felt he had been too outspoken against the South.

When the first official ballot taken in Music Fund Hall was counted, the surprise victor was John Charles Frémont. Many who supported his nomination argued that familiarity with the internationally famous explorer's name would influence undecided voters to support him.

Before he wrote a formal letter accepting the nomination, Frémont learned that he faced an undercurrent of suspicion and dislike. A majority of Democrats and some Republicans felt that he had antagonized the South by his public statements on divisive issues. A few in Republican inner circles tried to block his nomination by calling him a bastard. They charged that his hunger for money had led him to marry the daughter of Democratic Sen. Thomas Hart Benton.

Supporters of the man who had never held a political office pointed out that he had helped to win California for the United

John C. Frémont, famous as
"the Pathfinder," was a
major general early in the
Civil War. [LESLIE'S
ILLUSTRATED]

States. Although not presently significant, they suggested, the West Coast might some day be a potent force in national politics.

Keenly conscious of both pro and con views among the general public, Frémont's wording was carefully chosen in his letter of acceptance directed to "The National People's Convention at Philadelphia." Having already said that he would not campaign for the presidency, he promised soon to make clear his views "on the leading subjects now at issue."

Frémont was under no delusions. James Buchanan was all but certain to carry every southern state and some well above the Mason-Dixon Line. He had such solid backing at home that it would be hard to beat him in Pennsylvania. To win, Old Buck probably would need his own state, the South, and Ohio or Illinois.

Joel R. Poinsett, for whom the poinsettia is named, made young Frémont a protégé. [GEORGIA HISTORICAL SOCIETY]

SOME WHO knew him well agreed that Frémont was "unduly sensitive concerning his paternity." Having eloped with French-born John Charles Frémon, Mrs. Anne Whiting and her lover traveled through the South. When a son was born to them in Savannah, he was listed as a Georgian. When and why he modified his surname to Frémont is uncertain.

Good looking and adventurous, young Frémont studied in Charleston and came to the attention of Joel R. Poinsett. During his four-year term as U.S. secretary of war, the South Carolinian arranged for his protégé a choice place in which to work. Named to the U.S. Topographical Corps, Lieutenant Frémont assisted in surveying the route for a projected Charleston-to-Cincinnati railroad.

He spent only a short time in this work but developed a passion for exploration. Hence Poinsett sent him to join an expedition to the West led by J. N. Nicollet. The two men were so compatible that Nicollet took his young assistant with him when he went to Washington to supervise the mapmaking and to compile a report of his findings.

In the capital, Frémont met and was instantly smitten by fifteen-year-old Jessie Benton. Within a year they married, and

Jessie Benton Frémont met her future husband while in Washington with her influential father. [MISSOURI HISTORICAL SOCIETY]

Jessie's rich and powerful father arranged to send his son-in-law to explore the Oregon Trail.

Frémont demonstrated courage, skill, and determination of such high order that he later led four more expeditions. Kit Carson was his guide for two of them, and together they publicized the Great Salt Lake so effectively that Brigham Young selected it as a haven for the Mormons.

Having come to regard California as the land of opportunity, Frémont helped to wrest it from Mexico. In the process he gained possession of huge tracts of land that included the immensely valuable Mariposa gold mines.

Wealthy from land and gold, by 1856 Frémont was known universally as "the Pathfinder." Although lacking political experience, he was a natural choice to head the ticket in the first Republican try for the White House.

Before his nomination was certain, Frémont let it be known that Simon Cameron of Pennsylvania would be his choice as a running mate. Abraham Lincoln, who gained 110 votes for the vice presidential nomination in an informal poll of delegates,

In 1860 these campaign posters were made by pasting printed sheets on cloth. [LIBRARY OF CONGRESS]

was hardly known on the national scene. He lost to William L. Dayton but continued to be a faithful campaign worker for the Republican ticket.

THROUGHOUT THE North, special groups of Lincoln supporters who called themselves Wide-Awakes were organized. For practical purposes, Republicans put together the first national campaign organization. Lincoln took the lead in working for the support of Germans and other ethnic groups. Sen. Henry Wilson of Massachusetts headed the drive in the Northeast. In Pennsylvania, Cameron distributed leaflets that depicted Frémont as "a man of the people."

On election day one American in eight went to the polls. Massachusetts gave the Republican nominee a sixty-eight-thousand-vote margin. New York, Maine, Connecticut, Michigan, Ohio, New Hampshire, Vermont, and Wisconsin went into the Republican column.

Since Frémont's name did not appear on ballots in the South, Buchanan won the southern vote. Picking up Pennsylvania by eighty-three thousand votes, he knew he had won the White House when Lincoln and his allies lost both Illinois and Indiana.

Had Fillmore's votes gone to the Pathfinder, the nation would have had its first Republican president four years earlier. Since they did not, Buchanan's victory in the electoral college was much greater than in the popular vote total. Four years later, in 1860, the Democratic Party was splintered, guaranteeing that the second Republican nominee—regardless of who he might be—would take over both the White House and the American political spoils system.

29
Winfield Scott Hancock
A Yankee General Helped Fashion the Solid South

Benjamin Franklin Hancock, son of a Philadelphia seaman, was reared as a Quaker. Perhaps influenced by his famous name, he departed from the tradition of nonviolence when his son was born at Montgomery Square, not far from Norristown. Although knowing that some Quaker neighbors would be offended, Hancock named the infant for a soldier.

As a boy, his son was conscious that he was a symbolic successor to a revered leader. Later the head of the U.S. Army, Gen. Winfield Scott had first gained fame during the War of 1812. Some who knew the youngster who bore his name said that they considered it inevitable that their friend should become a professional soldier.

His name had little or nothing to do with the fact that by age sixteen "Win," as some called him, was a cadet at West Point. Fellow classmates included fellow Pennsylvanian George McClellan, U. S. Grant, James Longstreet, George Pickett, and Thomas Jonathan Jackson—later famous as "Stonewall."

During the Mexican War, Hancock was commended for action under Scott at Churubusco and Chapultepec, so he decided to make a career in uniform. At the outbreak of civil war, Captain Hancock was advanced two ranks and named a brigadier general of volunteers. Leading the Forty-ninth Pennsylvania Regiment and other units, he fought so skillfully in numerous battles that admiring subordinates began referring to him as "the Superb."

*Winfield S. Hancock looked
as if he had been cast in the
role attributed to him by his
nickname, "the Superb."*
[LIBRARY OF CONGRESS]

THAT LABEL was put to the test by a series of events that started late in June 1862. When they converged upon Gettysburg, neither men in blue nor men in gray knew that an all-important action was about to begin. Many analysts credit Hancock with having selected the field of battle on July 1.

Whether that was true or not, it was his force that stopped a July 2 Confederate attempt to move past the Federal flank. On the following day, it fell to Hancock to repulse Pickett's charge—a desperate attempt to penetrate the Federal center. Bombarded by what may have been the heaviest cannonade of the war, Hancock and his men held the line.

During fierce combat on the afternoon of July 3, the Montgomery County native was struck by a bullet from which he never fully recovered. Hitting the pommel of his saddle, the ball plowed into Hancock's thigh, taking with it a nail and large wooden splinters. Forced to the sidelines for a year, the semi-invalid was heartened to learn he was likely to receive the formal Thanks of Congress. The presentation was delayed, but when news of the coveted award reached Philadelphia, residents celebrated all day and all night.

Pickett's charge at Gettysburg was among the most celebrated and most futile actions of the war.

Back in action, Hancock accepted the surrender of the famed John S. Mosby and his rangers. Since that incident meant the Confederacy was doomed, Hancock rejoiced at his role in it. Commanding the Washington, D.C., garrison a bit later, he was forced into taking an action that he despised.

The four people sentenced to death for their participation in the assassination of Lincoln were consigned to the custody of the man with a Quaker heritage. That meant he had to arrange for their execution, including Mrs. Mary Surratt whom he considered to be a victim of hysteria and not a conspirator. Near the gallows on the grounds of the arsenal in southeastern Washington where the executions were to take place, Hancock poured out his revulsion:

> I have been in many a battle and have seen death, disaster, and victory. I have been in a living hell of fire and shell and grapeshot. I'd sooner be in the hell of battle ten thousand times over than to

give the order today for the execution of that poor woman. As a
soldier, I have however sworn to obey, and obey I must.

Soon made a major general, he was ordered South to head the
Department of Louisiana and Texas. There he acted contrary to
his orders, refusing to perpetuate a military regime that he felt
had outlived its purpose. His final insubordination consisted of
issuing General Order No. 40 soon after reaching New Orleans.
Recognizing the existence of a state of peace, it proclaimed that a
new system of justice would be observed. Those charged with
ordinary crimes not involving resistance to federal authority
would no longer be subject to military hearings. Instead, civil
courts would exercise jurisdiction over minor charges.

When news of his unauthorized action reached the capital,
many lawmakers reacted with fury. Some Radical Republicans
from his own state still demanded a fierce and lasting punishment of the South.

In Philadelphia, members of the famous Union League Club
took Hancock's portrait from a wall and consigned it to a
garret. U. S. Grant, who earlier had praised him with enthusiasm, protested that he strongly disapproved of his subordinate's actions. Relieved of command, Hancock was sent into
virtual exile in the Dakotas.

When the advocate of reconciliation returned to the East, he
was stationed at Governors Island, New York. Possibly affected
by his proximity to the powerful Democratic organization that
controlled New York City, in 1880 he accepted the party's nomination for the presidency of the United States.

His chief opponent, James A. Garfield of Ohio, was among
the congressmen most outspoken against General Order No.
40. When their bitter contest ended, Garfield had just 9,464
more popular votes than did Hancock. In the electoral college
it was a different story. Both men carried nineteen states, but
those that went for Garfield held the majority of votes in the
electoral college.

ANALYSTS WERE quick to point out that of the nineteen states
won by Hancock, most lay in the Cotton Belt. Alabama,
Arkansas, Florida, Georgia, Kentucky, Louisiana, Mississippi,
North Carolina, South Carolina, Tennessee, Texas, and Virginia

Cartoonists satirized presidential candidate Hancock as being under the control of Howell Cobb, symbolizing the Solid South.

went to the Democratic candidate. He also carried the Border States of Kentucky, Maryland, Missouri, and West Virginia.

Defeated in spite of the fact that Garfield was favored by less than ten thousand voters, Hancock was described as having "swept through Dixie like an autumn storm." A Union general from Pennsylvania had helped to create a longstanding electoral voting block famous as the Solid South.

30
Pontiac

The Leader of an Uprising Is Commemorated Everywhere

I give you warning, that if you suffer the Englishmen to dwell in your midst, their diseases and their poisons will destroy you utterly, and you shall die!"

Crossing the river into Pennsylvania, a chieftain claiming to lead New Jersey's Abenaki tribe was weary of giving up land. He said that he had received a message from the Great Manitou, who told him to spread it everywhere.

"Delawares, Senecas, and Shawnees have already taken up the tomahawk," he told all Native Americans who would listen. "Across the great mountains [the Alleghenies], near the mighty river [the Ohio], the Delawares are ready. They will be helped by our French friends, so lack nothing except a great warrior to lead them against the Englishmen."

Transmitted from tribe to tribe, this inflammatory challenge prepared the way for a young and daring chieftain to launch a series of coordinated raids. A small French fort stood near the point at which the Allegheny and the Monongahela Rivers unite to form the Ohio. The British, known to be eager to push westward, knew the strategic value of this three-river intersection. They would seize it and then all of western Pennsylvania would be in their possession, that is, unless a powerful leader could stymie their plans.

Many Native Americans already knew something of a warrior whom many said was invincible in battle. Born on the Ottawa River, Pontiac grew up in close contact with the French.

174

Pontiac as he was portrayed in
Harper's Encyclopedia of
American History.

As soon as he reached manhood, he announced his preference for them as opposed to the British.

His first daring exploit was as the leader of the Ottawas who helped the French to victory on the Monongahela River in 1755. Gen. Edward Braddock's raid directed against recently built Fort Duquesne was blunted by an ambush in which sixty-three British officers were killed or wounded. A tall lieutenant colonel from Virginia took command of the British force and managed to lead the survivors to safety. Later George Washington fulfilled the Abenaki prophecy by ousting the French and erecting Fort Pitt, which eventually gave its name to Pittsburgh.

Once Fort Pitt had been established, British colonists began to pour across the mountains in large numbers. The Delawares and Shawnees, who earlier had abandoned their tribal lands in Pennsylvania, were scattered along the banks of the Miami, the Muskingum, and the Scioto Rivers.

Eager to drive the newcomers back across the mountains, these tribes readily accepted Pontiac's leadership in a movement that his opponents later labeled a conspiracy. Soon the three tribes were joined by the Wyandotte, Chippewa, Fox, Winnebago, Ojibwa, and Seneca tribes.

Pontiac was a gifted politician and strategist. For the first time, the tribes were united under one person's leadership. Pontiac persuaded the previously warring tribes to focus on a single objective. Instead of organizing a typical raid against one target, he planned to strike at a dozen points at once. As a result, his opponents grudgingly called him the "Napoleon of the Forest."

In June 1763 he launched a massive wave of attacks along the frontier, focusing on those outposts that the British had taken from the French. Nine of them fell, and their garrisons were either killed or captured. Only three British posts withstood the assault—Forts Pitt, Detroit, and Niagara—and they were lonely bulwarks along a vast frontier.

Niagara was never attacked, and Detroit held out until the tribes abandoned their siege. From Philadelphia, Col. Henry Bouquet set out to relieve Fort Pitt, sure to be a target of the next uprising. He and his men spent two weeks at Carlisle assembling horses, oxen, wagons, and provisions. Soon the countryside proved too rough for wagons, so Bouquet resorted to 350 pack animals and pushed ahead.

Shortly after noon on August 1, the British clashed with the tribesmen at a small rivulet that became famous as Bushy Run. Knowing himself to be outnumbered, Bouquet executed a strategic move by which he defeated his opponents and lost only 115 men. Their spirit broken, the tribesmen fled from the field and took the news of their defeat with them. Two days later the rescue column reached Fort Pitt.

When word of the British victory spread along the frontier, Pontiac's Conspiracy collapsed. Far away in London, George III eventually sent Bouquet a formal letter of thanks. That was his only reward for having won a battle that many believe saved the unexplored half of British North America.

FUR TRADERS were thoroughly convinced that Pontiac's Conspiracy had been planned and launched from a tiny cabin in what is now Oakland County, Michigan. Furious when his allies gave up the fight against the British, Pontiac left the region and made his home on the Mississippi River. While visiting Cahokia tribesmen near today's East Saint Louis, he was killed by a warrior probably named Black Dog.

An Oakland County village near his Michigan cabin grew into a town and then into the city of Pontiac. Its proximity to

The Death of Pontiac, *by De Cost Smith.* [CONSPIRACY OF PONTIAC]

Detroit may account for the fact that the earliest major industry of the region was the Oakland Motor Car Company.

In 1925, after months of planning, Oakland executives were nearly ready to market a new light six-cylinder car. As yet the vehicle had no name, so a round of discussions was held. Some favored the name of the city which housed their plant; others objected vigorously.

"Pontiac is great," an advocate reputedly said, "but instead of putting the name of our city on the highway, it should commemorate the greatest of all Indian chieftains. He was the epitome of strength, durability, and ruggedness—the very qualities our new car has been built to exhibit."

Soon the Oakland-built automobile was formally named for the brilliant Native American who forged an unlikely military alliance. That left only one important thing for artisans to do; Pontiac must be depicted upon the new vehicle.

Numerous designs have been used since the first one, designed by William Schnell, appeared on the 1926–27 model. Unveiled at the New York Auto Show in January 1926 by Oakland, the "Chief

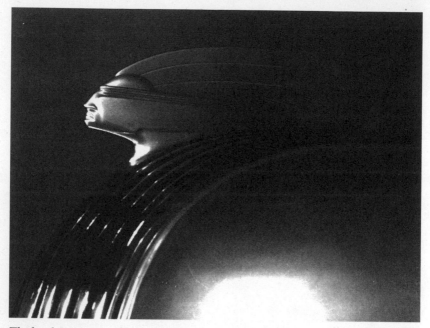

The hood ornament of the 1938 Pontiac automobile. [PONTIAC HISTORIC SERVICES, GENERAL MOTORS CORPORATION]

of the Sixes" was an instant hit. When 76,642 units were built during the sales year, it was apparent that Pontiac had returned and planned to stay. Soon the name of the chieftain supplanted that of the Oakland Company.

Numerous versions of his head and a few models of his entire body have been seen through the years. Adapted from a Jerry Farnsworth painting, the 1938 emblem is considered to be the most memorable of the entire series of emblems.

OSCEOLA, SITTING BULL, Tecumseh, and many other Native Americans are well remembered for their exploits and in the regions where they flourished. Their recognition, however, is less than that of the warrior whose scheme to master western Pennsylvania nearly succeeded. Millions of vehicles have taken the name of Pontiac everywhere and in car-conscious modern America have carved for him a unique niche.

31
Anthony Wayne
America's First Mutiny Did Little Damage

On the day that the British and the colonists fought the battle of Lexington, Massachusetts, the Keystone State enlarged its Committee of Safety. Dark-haired Anthony Wayne of Waynesboro, age thirty, became a member of this all-important body. When the residents of Chester County raised a regiment, Wayne became their colonel.

After distinguishing himself against the British in Canada, Wayne was made a brigadier general directly subordinate to George Washington. As commander of eight Pennsylvania regiments, he fought against Lord Cornwallis and at Germantown before leading his men to Valley Forge.

When they survived the winter of 1777, some Continental soldiers believed their troubles were nearly over. Few of them expected to fight for four more years, and none anticipated that the Pennsylvania general would have to deal with the first sizable American mutiny.

Camped in New Jersey three years after Valley Forge, two thousand men of the Pennsylvania line had plenty of reasons to complain. Most had not received the pay and bounties promised to them by the Continental Congress. Fast-depreciating Continental currency meant that even if the men were paid, their earnings were almost worthless. With some enlistments having expired and others due to do so soon, men eligible to go home were ordered to remain in service.

The winter of 1780 was far worse than what it had been when the army was encamped at Valley Forge. Men who had endured bitter cold and hunger finally rebelled at not receiving the pay promised to them.

The weather during December 1780 was far more severe than it had been at Valley Forge. Many soldiers had no shoes. Decent clothing was scarce, and blankets were thin with wear. Even the officers' morale was low.

In an effort to boost their spirits, the officers decided to have a banquet on the last day of the year. After drinking heavily, Colonel Humpton climbed on a table to toast his comrades who were about to go home.

While their wineglasses were raised, the sound of a musket shot came from a short distance outside. It was followed by another and another. Noises grew louder and more frequent, so a captain left the party to investigate. When he stepped outside, the officer realized that the simmering trouble had finally boiled over. Knots of angry men stood about talking and gesturing, many disregarding regulations and carrying their muskets.

The officers still enjoying their food and wine were startled to learn that their men were out of their huts. Humpton snapped a command: "Officers to post! Every man to quarters at once!"

When his order reached the milling crowd, the soldiers turned their backs and ignored it, laughing. Capt. Adam Bettin raised his hand to slap one of the insurgents but never finished his movement. With his arm extended, he fell, shot through the forehead by one of the Continentals.

By the time Capt. Samuel Tolbert and Lt. Nicholas White received nonfatal wounds, it was clear that the situation was out of control. Responding to an urgent message, Wayne galloped into the camp from the home in which he had been dining.

Stepping to the flank of the general's panting horse, Sgt. William Bowser took the offensive. Crying that he and his friends had been wronged, he said that they had decided to get what was due them by force of arms since they could get decent pay and clothing no other way.

Like every man in the camp, Bowser knew that a conviction of mutiny would carry a death sentence. Without wavering, he told his commander that they had no quarrel with him. Their anger, he said, was against the civilian authorities who had not kept their promises.

"We're making ready to head for Philadelphia, thirteen hundred strong," Bowser concluded. "Don't try to stop us; we're taking along half a dozen pieces of field artillery." He made it clear that if the men's demands were not met, they might take Philadelphia and put a torch to the city.

Determined to have a showdown with President Joseph Reed and the Supreme Executive Council of the colony, the men formed ragged columns and prepared to get under way. Unharmed and not having been threatened, Wayne faced a particularly difficult situation.

He had dealt with dissidents at Ticonderoga, but no other general in this war had been confronted with full-scale mutiny. To complicate the situation, he was aware that most grievances triggering the armed revolt were justified. Breaking with his long-standing record of closely following regulations, Wayne signaled that he would not try to stop the men in revolt. For once, he restrained his well-known fiery temper that had caused him to be called "Mad Anthony."

Surprised and delighted, the soldiers cheered their commander before setting off toward Vealtown with Wayne and a handful of aides following at a distance. Before settling down for the night, the mutineers dispatched messengers to Philadelphia.

Because of a temper that often blazed, Gen. Anthony Wayne became known as "Mad Anthony."

They resumed their march and on the third day decided to wait in Princeton for a reply from the officials who had received their list of complaints.

A messenger reported that Reed was coming to negotiate, so the mutineers did not resume their journey. Wayne soon agreed to serve as an intermediary in an effort to effect a compromise. Largely as a result of his efforts, major concessions were gained.

Many men had enlisted before January 1777; most promised to fight for three years or less, but others pledged themselves to stay in uniform for the duration of the war. Reed, head of the colony, authorized Wayne to circulate a solemn pledge. Under its terms, men who began their military service in 1776 could choose to stay and fight or they could withdraw from service. Troopers not eligible to make the choice were promised more and better clothing plus payment "as soon as humanly possible."

A grateful Congress presented Wayne with a special gold medal, recognizing his role in negotiating treaties with several Indian tribes and his expedition to Stoney Point during the Revolution. [HARPER'S ENCYCLOPEDIA OF AMERICAN HISTORY]

SOME OF his fellow generals were aghast when they heard how Wayne had handled the mutiny. Discipline had been abandoned, they charged. According to this point of view, the American Revolution was at the point of collapse.

Ignoring his critics, Wayne continued to command. Facing a smaller band of mutineers later, he dealt savagely with them and sentenced their ringleaders to death. Long after the Redcoats were defeated, he remained in uniform. After marching all the way to Georgia, he subdued the Creeks and the Cherokees before negotiating treaties with them.

Guided by Tecumseh and Little Turtle, he drove Native Americans far to the west. Below present-day Chicago he built a fort that became Fort Wayne, Indiana. Headed back toward his native state, he reached Presque Isle (now Erie) and found himself too sick and feeble to push ahead. One of a handful of men who fought the British from start to finish of the struggle, Wayne of Waynesboro had spent twenty-four years in the service of his country.

Knowing that his end was near, he reflected about his colorful and action-packed career. To aides he suggested that quelling the 1781 mutiny represented his finest hour. He was central in the quashing of a large-scale revolt without incurring any casualties. The mutineers received much of what they wanted, but not all.

None of them deserted to the British, a course of action George Washington feared most when he heard of the mutiny. Best of all in Wayne's view, a dozen regiments of combat veterans remained in the Continental army. If bungling by their general had caused them to go over to the British or to go home, the American Revolution might have faltered.

Part Five

Jigsaw Puzzles with Missing Pieces

Benjamin Franklin, deputy postmaster general of North America and London agent for Pennsylvania, New Jersey, Georgia, and Massachusetts.

32
William Franklin

New Jersey's Last Royal Governor

Tension between Great Britain and her North American colonies mounted long before the outbreak of war. From Maine to Georgia, some colonists rushed to take sides and others were eventually forced to do so. Those who favored armed revolt are honored as having been patriots.

Many colonists sided with the mother country and came to be called Tories or Loyalists. One of these was William Franklin, only son of the Sage of Philadelphia.

Born when Benjamin Franklin was twenty-three years old, William is regarded by some as constituting a stain upon the record of his father. Barely literate Deborah Reed seems to have been Benjamin's lover for some time before William was conceived, yet he did not marry her then or later. In spite of her strong dislike for the boy, she helped to rear him.

In polite society of the day, folk seldom referred to anyone as being illegitimate. Hence William, later formally adopted, was known as the "natural son of Benjamin." His father, who ran away from William's grandfather, soon became prosperous, then wealthy and famous. When William reached young manhood, Benjamin saw to it that he advanced rapidly in life, but his father's prestige was so great that his son was perpetually in his shadow.

Thanks to Benjamin's influence, William became a captain of Pennsylvania militia at age eighteen or nineteen. A few years

Possibly due to the use of a kite, artists often portrayed a small boy with Franklin during the lightning experiment. Some have named him William, but Franklin's son was grown at the time. [Fire Engine Panel]

later his father arranged for him to become comptroller of the general post office and clerk of the provincial assembly.

When William wasn't occupied with his duties, he spent much of his time with Benjamin. Hence it was natural for him to participate in his father's famous lightning experiments, somehow conducted without one or both amateur scientists being killed.

A few years later it was equally natural for William to accompany Benjamin to London when the one-time printer went there as agent of the Pennsylvania Assembly. They took lodgings at 7 Craven Street (later number 36) and remained there until returning to Philadelphia.

Although overshadowed by Benjamin, William made many friends among the rich and powerful men of his day.

Franklin's grandson and
secretary, William Temple.
[BRITISH MUSEUM]

One of them, William Strahan, wrote that to him the son
seemed "one of the prettiest young gentlemen I ever knew
from America."

Soon after reaching London, William followed his father's
footsteps and found a congenial female. She gave Benjamin a
"natural" grandson, but the name of William's lover is
unknown. Baby William Temple Franklin was named for his
father and the Temple Bar where he was a law student. Years
later he became Benjamin's efficient secretary.

LONG BEFORE reaching the English capital, Benjamin was so
admired that he was made a member of the Royal Society. Both
Harvard and Yale had conferred honorary master's degrees
upon him. Oxford University in England followed suit by
making him an honorary Doctor of Civil Laws just before he
returned to the colonies in 1762.

William had to be satisfied with an honorary master's
degree, but he earlier had gained other compensations for his
stay in England. Against the wishes of Benjamin, he married
wealthy Elizabeth Downes. An even greater coup was staged
when Lord Halifax, president of the Board of Trade, agreed to
speak to George III in his behalf. Because he was soon to be

appointed governor of New Jersey, the bridegroom-to-be remained in London after his father left.

Few days passed without some reminder that William was deeply obligated to his father. Without Benjamin's influence, he would have been given no well-paying appointments in Pennsylvania. When he reached age forty, it was for him that his father began his famous *Autobiography*. William knew that everyone knew he owed his Oxford degree and his governor's commission to his father's influence.

For years Benjamin readily lent money to his son, but this eventually became a major source of friction between them. In a constant stream of letters, the father prodded his son to begin repaying his debt.

WHEN THE long-expected break occurred between the colonies and the mother country, Benjamin was hailed as a leader of the Revolution. William clung so tenaciously to his Tory office and views that New Jersey patriots eventually put him under arrest.

After he had been in custody in New York for two years, his friends begged him to change his stance. William adamantly refused, insisting that although he was a prisoner of the revolutionists he was still the royal governor of New Jersey. Upon his release, he immediately sailed for England to claim the rewards promised him by the king.

Living in London upon a "half pension," or half the sum provided to veterans of Britain's many wars, William Franklin began asking friends to address him as "Sir." Some complied, but others preferred to call him "General" despite his lack of military experience.

Working as a self-appointed "agent for American Loyalists," he pressed many claims for compensation. Today we would classify his activities during thirty years as those of a lobbyist.

At age fifty-three, old by standards of the period, he broke the long silence between him and his father by writing a conciliatory letter. This led to a reconciliation, of sorts, as his father's eightieth birthday approached.

Although Benjamin was keeping a daybook, or diary, his entries concerning William are brief and infrequent. Their deep-seated political enmity seems to have pervaded every aspect of their lives.

As governor of New Jersey, William often sounded a theme from which he never varied after being ousted from office. He said he tried to hold the American colonies for England because he thought justice, right, and honor were on the side of the mother country. During his long self-imposed exile, he seldom mentioned Benjamin except when he apologized for being his son.

NO ONE knows if Deborah Reed was William's mother, and he revealed nothing at all about the mother of his own illegitimate son—not even her name. Until he gained favor at the court of George III, William wrote little about his political views.

Benjamin Franklin served in the Continental Congress and was a hard-working member of the Pennsylvania Committee of Safety, organized in the name of revolution. He helped to draft the Declaration of Independence and then signed it. When peace came, the new nation's senior statesman went to France as minister from the United States and with John Adams and John Jay negotiated a treaty of peace with Great Britain. At age seventy-nine he was a delegate to the convention in which the U.S. Constitution was framed.

With vital pieces of the puzzle missing, it is impossible to be sure why William took a course so far removed from that of his father. He may have had the genuine loyalty to England that he so fervently expressed. It is possible that he was motivated by hunger for power and the rewards that attach to it. A third possibility cannot be dismissed, however. Consciously or subconsciously, William may have harbored such resentment against overbearing Benjamin that he took the course of action best calculated to pain and to embarrass his famous father.

33

Mike Fink

Half-horse, Half-alligator, and King of the Keelboatmen

Whoo-oop! I'm the original iron-jawed, brass-mounted, copper-bellied corpse-maker from the wilds of Arkansas!

Look at me!

I'm the man they call Sudden Death and General Desolation! Sired by a hurricane, dam'd [mothered] by an earthquake, half-brother to the cholera, nearly related to the smallpox on the mother's side!

Cast your eye on me, gentlemen! And lay low and hold your breath, for I'm 'bout to turn myself loose!

As relayed to readers by Mark Twain in *Life on the Mississippi*, that challenge could have come from any of scores of men whose lives were spent upon the great river. Of them all, Mike Fink of western Pennsylvania was the undisputed king—if folk tales are to be taken seriously.

Probably of Scotch-Irish descent, Mike was born somewhere in the vicinity of Fort Pitt (modern Pittsburgh). He made his appearance close to the time the census of 1770 revealed that the thirteen American colonies had grown to 2.2 million in population. Any time he was asked about his name, he said it was Phinck—but even those who believed him preferred the simpler spelling.

His name really didn't make much difference, since before the age of twelve he was generally called "Bang-All." That nickname stemmed from his readiness to bang away with a musket at anything or anybody. He killed deer and otter with one shot but mostly missed humans because he just wanted to show them how close he could come without doing them any damage.

The Indian wars had dwindled to an occasional skirmish by the time Mike was wearing his first red shirt. Hunters had killed off so much game a fellow couldn't make a good living from pelts, so at about age fifteen he went into the transportation business.

There were mighty few good roads, no known routes over some mountains, and lots of creeks and rivers without bridges. This meant that long-distance hauling was mostly by water. Steam wouldn't arrive for quite a while, so man-guided and current-moved flatboats, barges, and keelboats swarmed on every big river.

Soon after he took to the Ohio River, champion marksman and fighter Mike was boss of a vessel and three or so crew members. If Andrew Fink and his wife of Allegheny County were his parents, as some say, they must have been mighty proud to see their boy take charge of a keelboat and its load of gear. Maybe from the influence of the Dutch who were early colonists in New York, he shook his head when addressed as "captain" and told folks to call him "patroon."

Claudius Cadot, who hailed from somewhere in the Ohio country, worked as Mike's deck hand for a voyage or two.

He wasn't eager to ride a keelboat for day after day, but he had his eye on a nice piece of bottom land he couldn't get without some cash. Claudius saw nary a glimpse of glamour or romance in life on the river. Of Mike he wrote little except to say that he was as wild and reckless as they come. Any time their boat tied up at a dock, Mike headed for the nearest doggery (saloon), and he could find it by its smell.

Barges, long familiar on western rivers, were clumsy craft that usually moved in only one direction. Things changed when the keelboat came along, for its sharpened ends enabled it to move backward as well as forward. Perhaps forty feet long and seven feet wide, or eighty feet long and ten feet wide, these contraptions looked flimsy but could carry up to thirty tons of freight.

Designed to operate in as little as two feet of water, the keelboat could go practically anywhere and did. Except when in deep water with a good current, keelers poled their craft

By comparison with a flatboat, a keelboat was almost a luxury liner. [THE 1838 CROCKETT ALMANAC]

toward its destination. It was fairly easy to make it down-stream, even when water was low. Especially on the Missis-sippi, a fellow sometimes had a chance to catch a mess of fiddlers (young catfish) that could be fried for supper.

Going upstream was an entirely different matter; there was no time to do anything but push against the bottom of the stream as long as a fellow had breath in his lungs. Mike was quoted as saying that poling against a current was "like trying to climb a peeled sapling, heels upward."

Before steamboats changed river life forever, maybe as few as twenty-five hundred or maybe as many as four thousand keelboatmen spent their lives on what were then called the western waters. Most of them may have had sweethearts in three or four ports, but only Mike and a few others took on a wife. The demands of life on the river left no time for married bliss. To survive on a keelboat, a man had to have an iron stomach, great courage, and muscles of steel.

Small coal-burning steamers started plying the rivers in the 1820s and before long they put muscle-powered flatboats out of business. Keelers had ruled the inland waters for about sixty years, but they vanished in less than one-tenth that time. Once they were gone, legends about them began to circulate.

As stories and tall tales moved farther and farther from their source, they exploded in size. By the end of the century Mike Fink was at least as heroic a figure as Daniel Boone and Davy

In real life, Mike Fink never looked so neat and clean as he was portrayed by some artists.
[THE 1836 CROCKETT ALMANAC]

Crockett. Spinners of yarns transformed the son of Pennsylvania's western frontier into half-horse, half-alligator.

Circulated by word of mouth for years, a story about Mike Fink and the kicking sheriff found its way into print about 1895. According to it, Mike poled his boat into a little place on the Ohio not far from Louisville. There he swaggered into the only store, bought a bottle of white lightning, took a few swallows, and began to tell of his exploits.

Except for one dried-up little fellow, all of the loungers around the store guffawed at Mike's punch lines. Annoyed and then mighty mad, the keelboatman stamped the floor and yelled, "Calamity's a-comin'! I'm a Salt River roarer chockful o' fight, an' I—"

He didn't finish his boast, for the fellow who never laughed jumped high into the air and as he fell back toward the dirt floor hit Mike squarely in the forehead with his elbow. Pulling himself erect after having taken a dreadful fall, Mike waded into the stranger with all he had.

Both men soon stopped to get their breath, then took after one another again. Looking as though he had been hit by lightning or tossed by a tornado, for once in his life, Mike gave up a fight.

"Stranger," he puffed, "I have to tell you I can't do nothin' a-tall with a fellow who's tougher to chaw than buckskin."

"Sure 'nuff?" responded his opponent. "Shake hands with Ned Taylor. I'm the sheriff around here, and if you and your scum buckets don't get back on the river in ten minutes, I'll throw every one of you in the calaboose."

Heading for the door, Mike turned and responded, "Five times is enough. You're a snag, a riffle, and a sawyer all in one. From now on, I'll do my buyin' somewhere else."

That yarn is unique, because alone among Mike Fink tales it describes him as a beaten man. Most of the time, even when in a shooting contest with Davy Crockett, he came out on top without breaking a sweat.

Somebody is supposed to have looked him over one time, then demanded, "What makes you and the other keelboaters keep your thumbnails oiled and sharp as the claws of a hawk?"

Without batting an eye, Mike held up his hands and flourished his telltale nails. "Mister," he said, "we take these things along so we can feel fur a stranger's eye-strings and gouge the news out of him."

SCATTERED CLUES support the view that there really was a flesh-and-blood Mike Fink. The trail of evidence begins with the first U.S. Census of 1790, the Washington portion of Allegheny County. It continues through the brief recollections of Claudius Cadot and scattered references from other people who lived during the keelboat era.

Many pieces of the puzzle have never been found and are unlikely to turn up in the future. As a result, we know little about Mike Fink except that he was a Pennsylvanian who took to the river very early and ended as king of the keelboatmen.

34
George B. McClellan
A General Can Buck a President, But He Can't Win

An April 1861 artillery duel in Charleston Harbor launched the Civil War, and at the start the South was better prepared to fight than was the North. President Abraham Lincoln responded by calling for seventy-five thousand volunteers to serve for three months. To the chief executive, ninety days seemed ample time to put down what he called an insurrection rather than secession of the Cotton Belt states.

On May 14 the president drew up a list of men he wanted the Senate to confirm as major generals. His choice of the date was not accidental, as Lincoln was meticulous about such matters. Exactly one month after Federal forces surrendered at Fort Sumter, he planned to elevate commanders whose swift and decisive action would soon bring the rebels to their knees.

Lincoln initially planned to ask that George B. McClellan and Joseph K. F. Mansfield be made major generals in the U.S. Army. For career soldiers, this rank carried with it the command of about fourteen thousand troops and the highest prestige. Benjamin F. Butler was to be nominated as a major general of volunteers, leading men whose term of service was limited to three years.

For reasons he never explained, the chief executive revised his request before it went to the lawmakers. Butler was nominated as planned and was confirmed; Mansfield's name was crossed out and he was made a brigadier general. McClellan was nominated as planned and had no difficulty in winning confirmation. He reached the capital immediately after the Federal disaster in the battle of Bull Run and assumed command of the military Division of the Potomac that included most of the Union forces.

Both the new major general and his president were immensely pleased. Ambitious, intelligent, and experienced, McClellan expected to make long-range plans for a Union victory. Still angry because of the Federal defeat at Bull Run, Lincoln was sure that a series of small successes by McClellan in western Virginia pointed to an immediate large-scale win.

A PHYSICIAN'S son who was born in Philadelphia, McClellan had an impeccable record. At age sixteen he withdrew from the University of Pennsylvania to accept an appointment to West Point. Four years later he graduated second in the Class of 1846, a class that produced twenty Civil War generals.

After winning honors in the Mexican War, the professional soldier from the Keystone State taught at West Point for three years. Although peacetime promotions were slow, he won his bars by the time he was twenty-six years old. Captain McClellan was one of a handful of carefully selected officers who went to Europe as an observer of the Crimean War.

Back home he soon expressed disappointment that he was not rewarded with another promotion. Resigning from the army in 1857, he became chief engineer of the Illinois Central Railroad. Rapidly moving up to the post of vice president, he then went to Cincinnati as president of the Ohio and Mississippi Railroad.

When it was clear that the North and the South were about to fight, both New York and Pennsylvania hoped to gain his services. He was leaning toward his home state when fate took a hand. As he was headed for Harrisburg to consult with Gov. Andrew G. Curtin, his train stopped at Columbus, Ohio, where he was met at the station by Gov. William Dennison. During their conference the chief executive of the Buckeye State persuaded him to head all of its militia and volunteer forces.

It was as a major general of Ohio volunteers that the man from Philadelphia led an army into the mountains of western Virginia, now West Virginia. He struck swiftly and decisively, defeating one Confederate leader after another—Robert E. Lee included.

Gen. George B. McClellan, "the
Young Napoleon." [LIBRARY OF
CONGRESS]

EVERYTHING IN his record suggests that as head of the Army of
the Potomac and the division that included it, he should have
achieved lasting fame. That he did not is usually attributed to
his reluctance to engage the enemy in battle.

Uniquely gifted in winning the confidence and loyalty of his
followers, McClellan was a man of tremendous energy. Few
observers were surprised at the November announcement that
Lincoln had made him general in chief, replacing the aged Lt.
Gen. Winfield Scott. That put him nearly at the top of the pyra-
mid of command, subordinate only to the commander in chief,
the president of the United States.

Almost from the start of McClellan's leadership, he and the
president were at odds. Their differences were so great that
Scott's replacement was in turn relieved after just one year.

Long before that, his men were affectionately referring to
him as "Little Mac." His treatment in the press, however, was
such that civilians typically scoffed at him as being "the Little
Corporal of Unsought Fields" or "Mac the Unready."

Committed to saving the Union, Abraham Lincoln wanted no delay. [NATIONAL ARCHIVES]

Many commentators about his brief period of top leadership consider the civilian nicknames to have been appropriate. A typical analysis holds that McClellan, "overestimating the strength of the enemy and underrating his own condition, refused to move."

HIS DIFFICULTIES during 1861–62 and the subsequent disparaging appraisals of him stem from a single factor. Like a mule that balks at doing its master's wishes, McClellan stubbornly resisted the will of the president.

Lincoln repeatedly made his impatience clear. He wanted immediate action. When McClellan objected to hasty movement, he was scolded. "Time," the president stressed over and over, "is the question which cannot and must not be ignored."

The differences between the two men were soon apparent throughout the North. Instead of publicly supporting McClellan, the president was quoted as having described his general in chief in four words: "McClellan has the slows."

Always conscious of anniversaries of events from both the recent and the distant past, Lincoln saw the approach of Washington's birthday as a decisive date. On January 27, 1862, his General War Order No. 1 required "a general movement of the Land and Naval forces of the United States against the insurgent forces" on February 22.

To make sure that he was obeyed, Lincoln added a warning to the effect that "the Heads of Departments, and especially the Secretaries of War and of the Navy, with all their subordinates; and the General-in-Chief, with all other commanders and subordinates, of Land and Naval forces, will severally be held to their strict and full responsibilities, for the prompt execution of this order."

Nothing significant took place on February 22, 1862; it was impossible to obey the directive of the commander in chief.

THIS IMPASSE between the civilian without military training or experience and his chosen general in chief is crucial in assessing George B. McClellan. Always stressing time, Lincoln wanted his forces continually on the offensive. In a message to the special session of Congress that convened on July 4, 1861, he promised a quick end to the war. That goal was dominant during succeeding months in which McClellan appeared to drag his feet deliberately.

His reluctance to move was based upon a conviction that time was on the side of the Union. Time would permit full mobilization of the Union's massive manpower. Time would permit expansion of industry so that weapons, ammunition, uniforms, tents, and a myriad of other military things could be provided promptly and in full.

Therefore Lincoln became impatient with his general in chief and then grew sufficiently angry to reduce his authority before dismissing him. Night and day were hardly more different than the attorney from Illinois and the professional soldier from Pennsylvania.

THERE IS no way to hazard a meaningful guess as to how long the Civil War would have lasted had McClellan's point of view prevailed. Vital components of the jigsaw puzzle are missing, for McClellan was removed before his ideas could be tested.

Because he challenged the views of a president whose assassination boosted him to a special kind of immortality, the Pennsylvanian is generally downgraded. It is possible that had McClellan prevailed, many of the 623,000 who died during America's deadliest war might have gone home to their wives and their sweethearts.

35
Ulric Dahlgren

Jefferson Davis and Richmond Survive a Fiendish Plot

Edward W. Halback, a teacher who doubled as a company commander of Virginia militia, ran his eyes hastily over documents just handed to him. At first they seemed to be routine orders issued by some Federal officer.

"William," he demanded while marking a spot on a page with his thumb, "where did you get these papers?"

"Off the Yankee I searched at the crossroads," responded the thirteen-year-old student who had recently joined the home guard. "I didn't do anything wrong, did I? He was shot in the back, and nobody had looked him over."

Halback assured him, "Far from doing anything wrong, son, you have been a player in perhaps the most important game of the war. I want you to be the first to hear part of what is written here. Listen and tell me whether you know what this means: 'We will cross the James River into Richmond, destroying the bridges after us and exhorting the prisoners to destroy and burn the hateful city; and do not allow the rebel leader Davis and his traitorous crew to escape.'"

"Sounds like the Yankees planned to take over Libby Prison and maybe Belle Isle [prison], too. Might have done it, if they hadn't walked into our ambush."

"You're right, William," Halback agreed, "but that was only part of the fiendish plot. When the Yankee officers were

203

Jefferson Davis and members of his cabinet were targets of the Kilpatrick-Dahlgren raid that failed.

released from prison, they were supposed to burn Richmond. That's not all; they planned to kidnap or kill President Jefferson Davis and members of his cabinet."

DOCUMENTS FOUND on Ulric Dahlgren created a sensation when the news was released to the Confederate press. Soon the *Richmond Examiner* reprinted the captured orders in full and identified the slain officer as the son of U.S. Rear Adm. John A. Dahlgren, famous for his invention of a heavy naval cannon. A news account with the published documents summarized the military action that led to their discovery.

Hoping to bring the Civil War to a speedy end, Gen. Judson Kilpatrick planned to strike Richmond without warning. Leading a band of veteran horsemen, the Federal officer crossed the Rapidan River and then the South Anna. Moving rapidly under cover of night, he was less than four miles from Richmond before he came under attack.

Forced to retreat, Kilpatrick and his men spent the night of March 2, 1864, about six miles from the enemy's capital. Resuming his northward march on the following morning, he lost about 150 men before reaching a place of safety.

*Col. Ulric Dahlgren led
raiders toward Richmond
despite having recently
lost a leg in combat.*
[LOSSING'S PICTORIAL
FIELD BOOK]

During his retreat Kilpatrick did not know that a small unit from his command, seeking to encircle Richmond and then enter it, had run into a hornet's nest close to the hamlet of Stevensville about 11:30 P.M. Ordered by unseen foes to halt, about ninety men in blue tried to bolt and run. Many who tried to escape were wounded while some of their comrades hastily surrendered.

Their leader, said the newspaper account, was struck five times. Equipped with a wooden leg that he had not yet learned to use skillfully, Dahlgren was limping along on crutches. Apparently having been an easy target, he fell early in the action and lay there as the fight moved away. Because of the damning letters, that may have been the most unusual raid staged during four years of conflict.

Richmond papers reached New York during the night of March 4. Horace Greeley, perhaps the most famous editor in the nation, found a copy lying on his desk when he went to his office at the *New York Tribune* on the morning of March 5. The more he read the more furious he became. Soon he dashed off lines later reprinted in his account of what he called "The American Conflict."

Adm. John A. Dahlgren, Ulric's father, stoutly denied that the signature on the damning papers was that of his son. [H. WRIGHT SMITH ENGRAVING]

Referring specifically to the documents already being called the Dahlgren Papers, Greeley wrote:

> These papers were Rebel forgeries, and the arson and murder they mention are Rebel inventions. These are intended to "fire the Southern heart," and justify murder by a pretense of retaliation.
>
> No Confederate newspaper has yet confessed that on the night in question authorities placed several barrels of gunpowder under Libby Prison. It is entirely beyond dispute that in case our brave men made a successful attack, Rebels would blow some thousands of captive Union officers into fragments.

Where Greeley received his information about the plot to blow up a prison, no one knows. He soon admitted that his account was based on false information.

Far to the south, the Pennsylvania officer and inventor whose son was the central figure in the Dahlgren Papers eventually received photographic copies of them. He took one look and denounced them as obvious forgeries; the signature, he said, was clearly not Ulric's.

ALTHOUGH SOUTHERNERS insisted that the papers were genuine, for many years northern leaders labeled them as the work of a clumsy forger. They based their conclusion upon the photographs, as only high-ranking persons ever saw the original documents.

Some of those who actually handled the Dahlgren Papers pointed out that they were difficult to decipher. Whoever the writer was, he used paper so thin that at some spots ink oozed from one side to the other. This aspect of the pen-written orders was especially noticeable in the writer's signature.

In 1879 former Confederate Gen. Jubal Early studied the documents carefully. At some points, he reported, "reverse" writing on the back side of a page could be read by means of a mirror. He theorized that the pen used to write words on the side of the page directly opposite the signature might have been too heavily inked. If that was the case, the ink might "bleed through" and cause the signature to seem bogus. Since he believed this to be the case, Early pronounced the papers to be genuine.

Marsena Patrick, a former Union general, took a different route to reach the same verdict. Capt. John McEntee, who was with Dahlgren on the night he was killed, was questioned at length by Patrick. The papers were genuine, said McEntee, because their message "corresponded with what Dahlgren told him."

Placed in storage and shifted from place to place until records about them were lost, the Dahlgren Papers turned up after many decades. Experts at the Library of Congress examined them carefully and reported that no evidence of forgery or tampering could be found. They believed in March 1864 there really was a scheme to burn Richmond and to kidnap or to kill Davis and his top aides.

NO ONE has ever found any hard evidence implicating any Federal officer who outranked the man killed near his target. If such evidence ever existed, it may have been destroyed when news of Dahlgren's death was made public.

Then and now, military experts say they are sure that a mere captain from Bucks County could not have staged the Dahlgren raid without authorization. If that verdict is right, the full story of the Dahlgren Papers would implicate a person or persons high in the Lincoln administration.

This puzzle from which vital pieces are missing has still another aspect. Sensational reports about the Dahlgren Papers in Confederate newspapers almost certainly reached an actor who was only slightly less famous than his brother.

Did word about the plot to seize or to slay the president of the Confederacy persuade John Wilkes Booth to frame a similar scheme? Possibly it played a part in Booth's plan to kidnap Lincoln and hold him as a hostage to demand that the shooting stop. If all the pieces of the puzzle were available, we would know. Unwittingly, an otherwise obscure captain from the Keystone State may have influenced the first presidential assassination.

36
The Whiskey Rebellion
Frontier Prelude to National Tragedy

Aroused and alarmed, members of the Pennsylvania Assembly turned to Albert Gallatin. Under his leadership the lawmaking body drafted a series of resolutions directed to the U.S. Congress. When these were put to a vote, forty men supported sending a strongly worded protest and only sixteen opposed this action.

A congressional bill sponsored by the U.S. secretary of the treasury, Alexander Hamilton, proposed that a federal tax be imposed upon "distilled spirits." Gallatin's Pennsylvania resolutions warned that if enacted into law, the tax would be "subversive of the peace, liberty, and rights of the citizens" of the brand-new nation.

By a vote of thirty to twenty-seven the New York convention ratified the U.S. Constitution on July 26, 1788. With eleven states having approved the document, the new national government came into being on March 4, 1789. Not quite two years old when confronted by Pennsylvania, the nation's challenge from a state was produced by the issue of "direct taxation."

Britain's tax upon tea, a contributing cause of the American Revolution, was still fresh in the minds of common folk. As recently as 1774 the First Continental Congress, meeting in Philadelphia, had branded any excise tax upon any commodity as "the horror of all free States."

Hamilton and his supporters faced a dilemma. They knew that the proposed tax on whiskey would lead to popular resentment

*Alexander Hamilton, U.S.
secretary of the treasury,
needed to find a way to address
the debts of the young nation.
The idea of a tax on whiskey
prompted a rebellion.*

that could trigger forceful resistance. Yet something had to be done about the finances of the infant United States of America.

Numerous colonies, now states, had gone deeply in debt to finance their roles in the Revolution. There seemed no hope that they could repay obligations of more than $24 million. Thus, against the opposition of future president James Madison, Hamilton persuaded the federal lawmakers to endorse assumption. Under this process, debts of the new states were "assumed" or taken over by the central government. In 1791 the national debt stood at what was then an astronomical figure—$75,463,000.

Hamilton's concern over the national debt caused him to lead the fight for a source of revenue in addition to tariffs upon imported goods. After pondering alternatives, Congress proposed a tax upon a commodity not needed to sustain life. The levy on whiskey became law on March 3, 1791.

As soon as Pennsylvania lawmakers again assembled, they directed resolutions to their congressmen and senators, directing them to try to prevent enforcement of the bill branded as "militating against the rights and liberties of the people."

THE SPRING of 1791 saw "trouble in River City." Having grown to a population of more than one thousand, Pittsburgh was the commercial and financial center of the four counties—Allegheny, Fayette, Washington, and Westmoreland—that were cut off by the Allegheny Mountains from the rapidly developing East. At least seventy thousand people were believed to live in that area. Only a few primitive roads, dotted with rugged mountain passes, ran toward Harrisburg and Lancaster and Philadelphia. This situation contrasted sharply with that of the eastern part of the state.

A sturdy type of wagon developed by the Mennonites in the Conestoga Valley near Lancaster was already proving its worth. With a sixteen-foot bed, this merchandise-carrier could bear loads of twenty-five hundred pounds or more. Wheels five or six feet high, equipped with four-inch iron tires, easily rolled through mud and over thickets. Benjamin Rush of Philadelphia was almost rapturous about this "ship of inland commerce" that helped transform the regions east of the Alleghenies.

Nevertheless, neither Conestogas nor any other vehicles could take merchandise from Philadelphia to Pittsburgh. There was a great deal of talk about building canals, but significant action lay far in the future. Merchandise flowed through the state from west to east only on the backs of pack animals.

Much land in the counties around Pittsburgh was so rich that farmers nearly always brought in fine crops, especially of rye. Since there was no way to get grain to market, growers reduced its bulk by turning it into whiskey that could go east in kegs. In the transmountain counties home-brewed alcohol had been a staple long before Continental soldiers won the freedom of the colonies.

"If Congress puts a four-cent tax on a gallon of whiskey, it will ruin us," agreed farmers who learned about the measure. Soon they discovered the terms of the act of March 3, 1791. It called for whiskey makers to pay a graduated tax that could go as high as eleven cents a gallon.

When the full effect of the federal law was realized, farmers banded together to resist the collection of the tax. Revenue officer Robert Johnson was tarred and feathered, and his colleagues realized what angry farmers were capable of doing to protect their industry. Gen. John Neville, chief inspector of alcohol

Just as the patriots had resorted to tarring and feathering royal agents collecting taxes on tea, the practice came to be applied to federal revenue agents.

production in the western counties, later received death threats. Whiskey Boys, as they called themselves, eventually burned his mansion, carriage house, and barns to the ground.

An informal protest organization gradually grew in size and clarity of purpose. Its initial three thousand members made themselves heard loud and clear wherever whiskey was produced. Other Pennsylvania dissidents were joined by some from the Cumberland Mountains and from western Virginia.

Announcing that Congress had no authority to impose the tax, in 1794 twelve thousand or more armed men set out to make the whiskey tax null and void. If necessary, they said, they would overthrow the federal government that threatened their livelihood. Led by David Bradford, they took control of Pittsburgh without resorting to violence. Yet they promised that they would declare the independence of western Pennsylvania rather than pay the tax.

By then it was clear that a genuine Whiskey Rebellion—not simply a noisy rural protest—was in progress. George Washington, who paid the tax on whiskey produced by stills he operated, viewed the Pennsylvania uprising as striking at the very heart of the young nation.

As a result, he requested and received congressional authorization to call out the militia of states close to the hot spot. Companies of militia from Pennsylvania, Virginia, and New Jersey soon began converging upon Carlisle. On August 7, 1794, Washington issued a proclamation ordering the insurgents to disperse by September 1. In a ceremony that caused apprehensions among the veterans of the Revolution, the president formally reviewed about fifteen thousand militia.

Governors of the three states providing troops were given military commissions, and with Washington briefly at their head, they set out toward Pittsburgh. By the time the federal force reached the Monongahela River, the Whiskey Rebellion collapsed without a skirmish being fought.

Bradford escaped and fled to Louisiana, but twenty leaders of the movement were arrested and sent to Philadelphia for trial. Two ringleaders were convicted of treason and sentenced to die. Neither went to the gallows, however, since the president pardoned them and their followers, who were convicted on lesser charges.

Federal experiments in raising revenue by means of excise taxes were far from over. Before the end of the century, Congress tried to reduce the national debt by taxing carriages. This predecessor of today's tax upon automobiles and trucks was soon dropped. So was a 1798 tax based upon the number and size of windows in a house.

This time, the revolt centered in southeastern Pennsylvania. Housewives dumped pots of hot water upon revenue agents sent to count and measure windows, causing the authorities to lose the little-known Hot Water Rebellion.

After enforcement of the whiskey tax became effective, it yielded only four hundred thousand dollars per year. Cost of collecting it ran to one hundred thousand dollars a year and reduced the national debt by only a trifle. As a failed fiscal experiment, it was of minor significance.

Personnel changes ended the hated revenue measure. Thomas Jefferson, the new president, had long opposed Hamilton's policies. Gallatin of Pennsylvania now accepted Jefferson's invitation to become secretary of the treasury. Together, they saw to it that the excise tax on whiskey was repealed.

The abolition of the hated tax should have ended the impact of the Whiskey Rebellion, which fizzled out when the militia became ready to use its muskets against farmers. That it did not is due to events that occurred halfway through the following century.

SOUTH CAROLINA and other Cotton Belt states announced their secession from the Union when the nation's first Republican president was elected. Initially labeling themselves independent republics, the insurgent states held that federal installations within their borders belonged to them. As a result, state militias seized forts, arsenals, revenue cutters, and branches of the U.S. Mint.

By April 1861 Fort Sumter in Charleston Harbor loomed to tremendous symbolic importance because it was the focus of the state-federal contest. An artillery duel led to the surrender of the federal installation on Sunday, April 14, 1861.

Abraham Lincoln had hoped that the defenders of Fort Sumter would be strong enough to hold out, but at least a month earlier he realized that military action was an option. Hence on March 18 he drafted a proposal to establish a Militia Bureau under federal control.

The attorney general, Edward Bates, quickly reported that the president did not have authority to set up such an agency. It would require congressional approval and provision of operating funds, ruled the top legal authority in the executive branch of government.

Many chief executives would have accepted an attorney general's opinion as final. Perhaps because he was a veteran of the courtroom and was committed to saving the Union by whatever means it might take, Lincoln persisted.

If it became necessary to put down secession by force, the tiny U.S. Army couldn't possibly do the job alone. Tens of thousands of men in state militia companies would be needed.

What federal action or nearly forgotten statute could serve as a peg, however flimsy from a legal standpoint, on which to hang a call for troops?

If any memoranda or letters passed between the White House and attorneys such as David Davis of Illinois and James Speed of Kentucky, they have vanished. If the president himself pored over statute books, he left no account of this activity.

At least one thing Lincoln did is a matter of record, however. On April 6 he conferred with four governors about the military status of militia units—all of which were under state rather than federal control. Significantly perhaps, one of the state executives who went to the White House that day was Andrew Curtin of Pennsylvania.

Logic says that the veteran attorney from the Keystone State was familiar with the course of the Whiskey Rebellion. Simon Cameron of Pennsylvania had just assumed his duties as U.S. secretary of war. He too knew that Washington had used state militias to disperse rebellious farmers sixty-seven years earlier.

There is no certainty that Lincoln questioned Curtin or Cameron about the Whiskey Rebellion. It is clear, however, that from one of them or from other sources or through his own research he came to see it as vitally important. Here was the key that could unlock the gates between the states and the central government!

Relying upon measures taken to quell the Whiskey Rebellion, one day after the surrender of Fort Sumter Lincoln called for seventy-five thousand militia to serve three months under federal control. Since his proclamation clearly meant armed conflict, previously wavering states hurried to secede. The Confederates mustered their militia and volunteers to meet what they considered to be a federal threat. Knowing that militias now under his control must fight within ninety days or go home, Lincoln pushed for action that precipitated the battle of Bull Run in July 1861.

Throughout the world, the years 1861–65 are famous—or infamous—as the most costly in American history in terms of the number of casualties. Yet no one can fully explain the beginning of the Civil War; important segments of the puzzle are missing.

Who first suggested that Lincoln base his call for militia upon suppression of the Whiskey Rebellion is a matter of conjecture.

A bloodless artillery duel at Charleston, South Carolina, triggered a call for seventy-five thousand militia by Abraham Lincoln. [HARPER'S WEEKLY]

Another riddle cannot be answered: Had Pennsylvania farmers not protested the whiskey tax so violently that militias were assembled, would a potential civil war have fizzled out for lack of troops to fight for the Union?

Albert Gallatin is the subject of chapter 3.

Index

Boldface page numbers indicate illustrations.

Unless the name of a country or state follows that of a county, city, or town, the listing indicates a Pennsylvania site.